Private O'Neil

Private O'Neil

The Recollections of an Irish Rogue of
H. M. 28th Regt.—the Slashers—During
the Peninsula & Waterloo Campaigns
of the Napoleonic Wars

Charles O'Neil

LEONAUR

Private O'Neil: the Recollections of an Irish Rogue of H. M. 28th Regt.—
the Slashers—During the Peninsula & Waterloo Campaigns
of the Napoleonic Wars
by Charles O'Neil

First published in 1851 under the title
The Military Adventures of Charles O'Neil

Published by Leonaur Ltd

Material original to this edition and its publication
in this form copyright © 2007 Leonaur Ltd

ISBN: 978-1-84677-172-9 (hardcover)
ISBN: 978-1-84677-171-2 (softcover)

http://www.leonaur.com

Publisher's Notes

Contents

Preface

The history of times and events, of men and their characters, must ever be replete with interest and instruction. Chronicles of the great and wise, the noble and the learned, are often presented to the world; and the military hero and chieftain finds everywhere his biographer. We read of campaigns that his mind has traced out, of battles which his plans have won; and we forget, in our admiration of his skill and power, those by whom the heroic deeds were done, the victory gained. Generals, says one author, "often calculate upon men as though they were blocks of wood, or movable machines." Yet every one of these nameless soldiers has feelings as acutely alive to suffering and to honour as those who look upon them thus.

It is well sometimes to turn away from the glare and tinsel of rank, from the glitter of arms and the pageantry of war, to follow the common soldier in his partings and wanderings, to cast the glance of pity upon his sufferings, and allow the heart to be moved with compassion while regarding the temptations which must ever beset his path. It is only thus that a true knowledge of the evils and miseries of war can be obtained; and only when this knowledge is spread far and wide, that we may hope to see the banner of peace unfurled, and the olive-branch waving in quiet, where now the sword spreads its desolation, and the vulture feasts on the unburied dead.

Thoughts like these may, perhaps, lend interest to the un-pretending narrative of one who now presents himself and the scenes of his times before an indulgent public, with none of the advantages of rank, or birth, or fame, to recommend him to its notice. Simply one of the rank and file, he was an actor and participator in the scenes he has endeavoured faithfully to represent.

It is his ardent wish, by this little volume, to awaken more interest in this class of his fellow-beings, so often forgotten in the lustre of that halo which rarely fails to surround the victor's name.

The work, such as it is, he cheerfully commends to the *public,* looking with unshaken trust to its kindness and sym-pathy for the success and encouragement which he hopes it may be his lot to meet.

Worcester
July 4, 1851

CHAPTER 1

I Take the 'Shilling' (More than Once)

People advanced somewhat in life, and surrounded by a family of children, often find great pleasure in retracing scenes of their own childhood,—in living over, again and again, the hours which have been to them so productive of happiness or misery; and the events of those bygone days present to their minds scenes of far deeper and more thrilling interest than the present can ever do. The thrice-told tale is as new, and as glowing with interest, as though its occurrences were but of yesterday. This is true in the case of most whose lives have been diversified by the changes of varied condition and prospects.

But how much more true is this of the old soldier,—one who, in early life, became inured to the hardships of war and the severe duties of camp life. Scenes in the camp, and on the bloody field of martial combat, where death, in its most terrific forms, is met by many,—the horrors of the siege, and the consequences to the vanquished,—the sufferings, the writhings and groans, of the distressed and the dying,—too deeply impress the mind to be ever erased; and, in our times of peace, should serve to enhance the value of the blessings we enjoy. It is, perhaps, with something like these feelings, that the author of the following sketch presents his narrative to the public. He can claim no titled ancestry, nor lordly birth, to throw around him a fictitious glory. This tale draws its interest from the wild scenes of war, and the wilder passions of men's souls, which it has been his fortune to encounter. It is his hope both to instruct and amuse the young, that they may better prize the blessings of peace; and learn that war, with all its glory, is to be dreaded, not sought for,—that it is productive of far more evil than good, even to the successful party, and that it should ever be, to all nations, only a last resort from the most flagrant oppression.

I was born in Dendolk, in the county of Lowth, Ireland, in June, 1793. I was the youngest of eleven children, six of whom were sons, and five daughters. My father's name was Charles O'Neil, and my mother's maiden name was Alice McGee. My father was a carpenter by trade, and he support-ed his large family by daily toil. He was an industrious and active labourer, and in other times would gladly have seen his family settle around him, pursuing the peaceful avocations of husbandry, or engaged in some of the useful mechanic arts. But it was our fortune—or misfortune, I should say—to live when all Europe resounded to the din of arms, and the glory of martial life, amid the confusion and carnage of battle.

Napoleon, the mightiest of heroes and conquerors, was then rapidly ascending to the zenith of his glory; and all the crowned heads of Europe, terrified by his growing power, and anxious to save themselves and their thrones, began to prepare themselves for resistance. Recruits were sought for in every village and hamlet. The honours of the soldier's life, and the glory of the military profession, were every-where, and by all classes of people, the topics of conversa-tion. Fathers and mothers were careful to instil into the minds of their children the glory and honour of a military life, and the fair young damsels of our own dear island— for Ireland has charming and beautiful girls—were scarcely willing to regard any young man as honourable or brave, who did not enlist, and aim to deserve well of his country.

He is a soldier, he has fought in such a battle, he belongs to His Majesty's regiment, &c, were a sure passport to society and respectability.

All other occupations were considered tame and spiritless, fit only for the aged, infirm, and for cowards. My father caught the spirit of the times, and although too old to engage in such an enterprise himself, gave his ready permission to Arthur, my oldest brother, who early sought to distinguish himself on the field of battle. My mother's consent was not so readily given, but even she did by no means object to his new enterprise; and when he presented himself before his parents, in his new uniform, for their parting blessing, she felt proud that her son was possessed of such a noble, courageous soul.

She cheerfully gave him her hand, saying, "Go, my son; cover, yourself with glory in the service of your country, and when you are old, you will be honoured, respected, and provided for." But, alas! how little did my mother think that the first news she would hear from her first-born son, after this blessing, would fill her own heart with grief unutterable.

He enlisted into the navy, and was placed upon a seventy-four gun-ship, named the *Terrible*; and terrible, indeed, it proved to him, for he was killed by a cannon-ball, a few months only after enlisting, in an engagement which took place in 1807, near the coast of Holland, between His Majesty's fleet and the French naval force. His death was a severe affliction to my parents, and completely damped my father's desire for military honour for his children. It was, therefore, with deep regret that they saw in my brother James' mind a growing dislike to the quiet duties and occupations of home, and an earnest longing for those warlike scenes which had been so fatal to Arthur.

This desire soon grew so strong that entreaties and persuasions were alike useless from my dear and aged parents;

and in less than two years from Arthur's death, he enlisted in the royal army of George IV., in the 96th Regiment of Foot. It was a sorrowful day in our little home, when the news came that his regiment was ordered abroad, into the foreign service. My father gave him much good advice, with many directions for the attainment of that honour he hoped to see him enjoy, at some distant day. But my poor mother could only weep, and express her deep regret that Jimmie would not be contented to live at home, at the same time reiterating her confident prediction that she should see his face no more.

Since the melancholy death of Arthur, the glory and honour of military life all gave place to the carnage, the slaughter, and the dreadful sufferings of the battle-field, where no kind hand could minister the slightest consolation, and where agony unmitigated might be the fate—and to her mind undoubtedly would be—of her son. She wept aloud, and would not be comforted. But the die was cast.; Jimmie was resolved, at all hazards, to be a soldier. He thought not of danger, and did not fear death. He only thought of the excitement of martial strife, the joy and honour awaiting the victor, and the subsequent reward. Alas! for him the bright future never dawned. My mother's fears were but too well founded; for he, too, fell dead upon the field of battle, while fighting bravely for his country, in his first engagement, in the bloody battle of Talavera.

It was my father's wish that I should become a carpenter; and he, early in life, put me an apprentice to his own trade. But the quiet habits, constant labour,—destitute of an exciting or romantic incident,—of a mechanic's life, ill suited the tastes I had already formed. There resided near us an old soldier, who found great pleasure in relating the adventures of his past life; and I was never weary of listening to them. My imagination was excited, and the romantic scenes he related to me, with the thrilling incidents of a soldier's life, made a deep and permanent impression upon my mind. Alas for me, that I ever fell in company with this old soldier! My peace was destroyed; I was uneasy, and determined not to remain in my employment, as a carpenter's apprentice. Each interview with him strengthened my desire for a participation in those scenes which, I was sure, would be so delightful and interesting.

Mingled with a desire to see foreign countries, and be a sharer of those actions to whose thrilling narration I had so often listened with so much interest, came an ardent thirst for revenge on those whom I regarded as the murderers of my brothers. About this time, one of my cousins, to whom I was warmly attached, resolved to enlist in a regiment that was then being formed at Belfast. He was very anxious that I should accompany him. It did not require much persuasion to induce me to determine so to do. But I remembered how difficult it had been for my brother James to gain my parents' consent, and being anxious to avoid a scene which must be so painful to all, I resolved to leave without their knowledge.

This was a most wicked resolution, and deeply do I regret such an unkind and unwise act. It was not without many misgivings and fears that I left the home of my childhood. O, that I never had stifled that voice which so clearly bade me not to go under such circumstances! There were many things to call up these misgivings, and to hold me back from such a cruel purpose. The uniform kindness of my parents, the severe trials to which they had already been subjected,—for, beside the loss of my brothers, they had buried four of their children, in early childhood,—their known wishes that I should pursue my father's calling, the affection I still felt for home and my dear parents,—all these made me hesitate, as I stood at our little gate, with my earthly all in the small bundle I held in my hand. There, on the one hand, were my dear parents and brothers and sisters, all quietly asleep, wholly unconscious that I had formed such a wicked purpose, and by stealth packed my few clothes, and whatever else I could call my own, in my little bundle; there was the home of my childhood, the hallowed scene of my early sports and joys, under the smiles and watchfulness of the kindest of parents; there were the early associates of my boyish days, and all necessary to render me happy and quiet;—and, on the other, were the glories of the military profession, and the unreal pleasures I had anticipated in foreign countries,—scenes and events pictured in my imagination from the stories of that old soldier.

The realities of home, and all that was dear on earth, opposed to the more heated imaginations of scenes in other countries, and upon the field of carnage,—I almost resolved to go back, and become what my parents wished. I hesitated, at that solemn and still hour of the night, for some time, before I could break away. Had I only gone back, and done what I knew I ought to have done, it would have been right; and I caution all my young readers never to stifle such convictions, or break away from such restraints.

But the thought of my cousin, who was waiting for me, and the glowing scenes which my imagination had painted in the countries beyond the sea, to which I hoped soon to go, drowned the earnest pleadings of the good spirit, whose still small voice was heard in my soul. I, with sudden violence, sundered these unpleasant reflections, and madly resolved, come what would, to go ahead. I rushed, with the utmost rapidity, from my home, and drowned every conviction and thought that would come up in my soul, of all that I had left behind. I soon found my cousin, and we pursued our way to Belfast, with the utmost rapidity.

How little did I then think that so many years would elapse before I should again see that well-known spot, and those dear friends who, in spite of my wildness and disobedience, had loved me through all, and were unceasingly seeking my best good! But I was now to enter another sphere of life, and be subjected to far other influences than those to which I had been accustomed from early childhood. I was at this time only seventeen years of age,—1810. My comrade, like myself, was quite young. Our ideas of the happiness of a soldier's life were much the same; and we amused each other, on our lonely way, by relating all the adventures either of us had ever heard, of what was then to be our future profession.

When morning came,—that morning in which there was to be so much grief in our quiet homes, and when the tears of my dear mother, and her groanings, were to be again heard, for an absent son, who had stolen away,—we feared to be recognized, by some one who might be passing, if we continued our journey. So we stopped in an old, deserted hut, and making our simple meal of the bread we had brought with us, we lay down and slept. About four o'clock in the afternoon, not seeing any one near, we pursued our way, and travelled all night.

The next morning found us far from home, among scenes and people entirely strange, and greatly fatigued by our night's march. We found a teamster, who was going to Belfast, and, by much persuasion and entreaty, succeeded in persuading him to carry us to that city. Right glad were we to rest our weary legs, and amuse ourselves by gazing at the new and strange objects which met our eyes as we passed along the road. We reached Belfast about sunset. Neither of us had ever before seen so large a place as this; and we thought, as we rode through some of its principal streets, that we never should be weary of gazing upon its churches and public buildings, which appeared to us so grand and beautiful.

This city is one of the principal seaports of Ireland. It lies about ninety miles north of Dublin, on the banks of the river Lagan. With a population of forty thousand, and all the advantages which it possesses for trade, it may well be imagined that we found in its busy streets and crowded thoroughfares enough to rally again all the excitement and glowing visions which our fatigue was beginning, in some degree, to dim. But when our driver stopped at a small inn, in one of the back streets of the city, a good supper and bed seemed too inviting to be resisted, and we were soon asleep.

At early dawn, however, we were awakened by the roll of the drum, and were soon in the street, gazing, with wondering eyes, at the many strange sights we saw. Near our hotel a canal came in, which connects the little lake of Lough Neagh with the Bay of Belfast. The canal-boats attracted our attention, and my cousin proposed visiting them; but, far over the tops of the houses, I could see the tall masts of the vessels which lay moored in the harbour, arid I could not restrain my curiosity longer. So we were soon on our way to the port. The harbour is an excellent one. It is constantly filled with, shipping, as vessels drawing thirteen feet of water can easily anchor here.

We had scarcely reached the wharf, when I was surprised to hear a familiar voice calling my name. Turning hastily, I discovered an old playmate, who had left Dendalk about three years since, for the sea. He belonged to one of the large vessels now in port. Nothing could have been more opportune for us, as he was acquainted with the place, and showed us the ship where he was, which we should not otherwise have had an opportunity of visiting.

To him we confided our object in leaving home, and he promised to aid us in finding the officer. Soon after leaving the wharf, we passed a large building, which, my friend informed us, was a manufactory for Irish linen, which is one of the staple exports of the place. I afterwards learned that no less than eight hundred looms found continual employment in the production of this valuable commodity. But much as I should have enjoyed a visit to this place, a scene now presented itself which had, in my eyes, far greater attractions.

Near the centre of a small open place stood a covered cart, embellished with flaming handbills, giving a description of the success of the British troops on the peninsula. On its top stood a neatly-dressed soldier, who was haranguing, with much earnestness, the motley group that surrounded him, and calling loudly for recruits to engage in such glorious service. Judging from the description we heard, our most sanguine expectations had fallen far short of the reality; and of course this was an opportunity not to be lost.

We eagerly pushed our way through the crowd, which we had some difficulty in doing; but the eagle eye of the officer soon rested on us, and, perceiving our eagerness, he called out, "Make way, make way there, my lads! that's right, that's right,—fine soldiers you'll be, my hearties, I warrant!" Of course, all eyes were directed to us; and if any idea of retreating had occurred, the loud hurrah for the new soldiers, which ran around the crowd, would at once have decided the question. But no such idea came to-disturb our peace, and our names were handed in. Being asked how long we would serve, each of us answered, without a moment's hesitation, "For life." "For life, then, are you soldiers of His Majesty," the officer replied.

Each of us then received from him eighteen guineas, and were sent to the barracks, as members of the 8th Regiment of Foot. Much elated with what we considered our good fortune, we proceeded at once to make a selection of our kit, as it is called. This consisted of two shirts, two pairs of stockings, a plate, knife and fork, and a few other small articles, the cost of which does not often exceed a guinea. A suit of regimentals was then provided for us, by the officer of our mess, and we soon found ourselves quite at home in our new situation. But we had not been here long, when we began to find the old adage applicable in our case, "All is not gold that glitters." The drills to which we were subjected were very tiresome to those as unaccustomed to any kind of restraint as we were.

In addition to this, as many of our troops had deserted, we were so closely watched that we lost all the enjoyment that I had anticipated in viewing the curiosities of the city. It was hardly to be supposed that, unwilling as I had been to submit to the quiet restraints of home, I should find a pleasure in the rigid discipline of the parade-ground; and before one week had passed away, I found myself pondering whether I could not, in some way, escape from my regiment. Not that I intended to give up the military profession entirely, for I still thought that in some other place I should find the happiness I sought.

Every night, after we had retired to our quarters, I listened to the many tales my comrades were ever ready to tell, of those who, weary of their lot as soldiers, had deserted,— of their hair-breadth escapes, and the cruel punishment to which they were subjected, when discovered. The very romance connected with the undertaking, and the thrilling interest that existed in listening to these adventures, strengthened in my mind my desire to share in their experience. It also occurred to me that should I still wish to continue in the service, I might go to another part of Ireland, where I was unknown, and again receive the bounty-money offered to all enlisting. Yet all these motives would have been insufficient, had not an incident occurred which aroused all the independence and opposition of my nature.

I was unjustly accused of a breach of discipline, and, in spite of my protestations of innocence, was punished for it. This circumstance was sufficient to overcome any fear that might exist of the consequences; and the very next day—

only twelve days from the time I had entered the service, with such glowing anticipations—an opportunity occurred, which I determined not to lose. Close to the parade-ground was a small shop where liquor was sold, and which was much patronized by the soldiers. Into this shop I saw an old clothes man enter, and immediately followed him. Having ordered a pint of porter for him, I asked him if he would be willing to exchange his old and ragged clothes for my new suit. He said he would, and informed me that I might meet him under a bridge near, where we might make the exchange. Observing that no one was near, I went under the bridge, and soon reappeared, dressed in his old clothes, and bearing his pack. Thus disguised, I walked bravely onwards, even passing some of my old comrades, who did not recognize me. The alarm was soon given, and soldiers started in pursuit. They soon came up to me, and even stopped to inquire if I had seen any one pass.

It was with no small degree of pleasure I saw them take another road from the one I designed to pursue. As soon as they were out of sight, I renewed my speed, feeling anxious to get as far as possible from Belfast before another morning. At length, wearied out, I solicited and obtained permission from a farmer to remain during the night. He observed me, however, so closely, that my suspicions were aroused, and I began to fear that he would attempt to inform against me, in order to obtain the reward offered to those who deliver up a deserter. lie questioned me quite closely, as to where I had been, where I was going, and, finally, asked me directly, if I had not been a soldier. I denied it at first, but soon concluded that my best way would be to appeal to the old man's generosity. I did so, and was not disappointed. He not only did not inform, but kindly offered to assist me on my way.

Before daylight we arose, and I dressed myself in a suit of clothes, with which he furnished me, and taking my seat by his side, in his market wagon, was once more on my way home. He talked to me long and faithfully on our journey, nor did he leave me until he saw me alight at my father's door. Good old man! I shall never forget his kindness. He has long since gone to his reward; yet at this distant day my heart throbs with the recollection of it, and I shall never forget the old farmer of the Downs.

My parents received their returning son with true parental affection, and to them I gave what money still remained from my enlistment bounty. When I first returned home, they earnestly hoped I should now be willing to remain there; and I might, perhaps, have yielded to their entreaties, could I have done so with safety. But soldiers were often passing through Dendalk, and I was in great danger of being recognized. This induced my parents to consent that I should leave home a second time, and try my fortune again in the camp. There was no lack of opportunity. A regiment was forming at Navan, and to this place I directed my steps, and soon found myself enrolled as a member of the 64th Regiment of Foot, and again received eighteen guineas from the service.

I had been here but three days, when we were summoned out to witness the punishment of a deserter. He was an athletic young man, who had been pressed into the service. He had left at home an old mother, a sick wife and one child, dependent on his daily labour for support. Finding all attempts to procure a discharge unsuccessful, he had deserted, and been retaken, through the treachery of a pretended friend, who, for the sake of a few pounds, could betray the distressed son and husband to so cruel a punishment, and a still more cruel separation from those so dearly loved. It would naturally be supposed that the strong temptation which existed for desertion might have mitigated the punishment; but this was not the case.

War recognizes none of those affections which make the happiness of the human heart. It seeks only to crush out their life, or perhaps holds them up to ridicule, as things of no moment. He was sentenced to receive three hundred lashes. His sentence was executed, and we saw him taken down, bleeding and mangled, and carried to the hospital almost insensible. It was a long time before he recovered sufficiently to perform duty, he did not again attempt desertion. A few days after, word was brought him that his wife and child had died from want, and that his old mother was in the parish workhouse. He was never seen to smile again. The soldiers were all kind to him, but I learned afterward, that he soon sickened, and died of a broken heart. The sight of this punishment filled me with dread, and threw quite a damper on my exalted ideas of a military life.

Our commanding officer was very strict,—unnecessarily so, as we thought,—in his rules, and rigorous in the execution of punishments. He had been so long in his situation, and seen so much of misery, that his heart was completely hardened. Every disobedience, even an accidental variation from his orders, however trifling, was punished to the extent of the law—often beyond it.

If I had found the discipline and restraint of Belfast unendurable, this was far worse. Nor was I at all disposed to submit to it. I had deserted once, without discovery. Why should I not do so again? I was restless and uneasy, and came in for my full share of punishment. I was thinking on this subject one day, when my attention was suddenly arrested by a conversation between two officers near me.

"How soon is the regiment expected from Belfast?" said one.

"In about three days," replied the other.

"Do you know its number?"

"The 8th Regiment of Foot," was the answer.

21

It was the very one with which I had been connected! Of course, I should be at once recognized, and not only lose the bounty-money I had already received, but be punished as a deserter. This dreaded prospect roused every energy of my spirit, and I resolved to escape before their arrival, at all hazards. Fortune seemed to favour my undertaking. The next morning, which was the 11th of June, only twelve days from my second enlistment, I was sent out, with a number of other soldiers, to bring back some horses which had strayed from the camp, having broken from their pickets.

On my way, my attention was accidentally attracted to a large tree, which grew near the road. The tree was hollow and its entrance was completely screened from observation by a luxuriant vine which twined itself around the trunk. As we were searching for the horses, I succeeded in examining it, without attracting observation, and found that I could be concealed there for a short time.

Taking advantage of a moment when no one was near, I placed myself in the tree, and, scarcely venturing to breathe, awaited the search which I knew would be made for me. Once or twice, a soldier passed so near that I could hear the leaves rustle against his coat. But their efforts were fruitless. I was not discovered, and remained in my shelter until the noise of their footsteps had died away. Then, creeping out, I ran as fast as I could away from Navan, avoiding as much as possible the highways, as I knew that my dress would betray me. It was necessary that I should rid myself of it as soon as possible; but there was great risk in doing it, as I should, of course, betray myself to the one with whom the bargain should be effected;—and, where all were strangers, I dared not run so great a risk.

I did not wish to go home, as the danger to which I was now exposed would be greater even than before, and would be a source of keen distress to my mother. So I directed my steps to my sister's cottage, which was much nearer than my father's. Here I met with a kind reception, and a secure hiding-place for some time, in return for which I bestowed the whole of my money on her. We had many conversations as to my future course. She was very anxious that I should give up my ideas of being a soldier, and go quietly home. But to this I could-not consent. I had, it is true, ascertained that there were troubles in that life, as well as in others; but I still thought that when I had once entered upon active service I should find my lot quite different.

I had as yet seen no foreign countries, nor could I bear the idea of settling down to a steady employment. I wanted a life of ease, excitement, and pleasure. I had heard far too much of that intense excitement which pervades every breast when the sound of the trumpet summons the soldier to combat, and of the glory that follows the successful warrior, to feel willing to give it all up. Beside, my condition was now irksome in the extreme. There was so much danger of being recognized, that I could not feel myself safe anywhere.

A description of my person and appearance had been sent all over the country, with the offer of the usual reward. I concluded that, should I enlist in another part of the country, I should stand a much better chance of not being recognized, as they would hardly look for a deserter in the barracks.

On the 3rd of July, therefore, I bade my sister a long farewell, and started out in pursuit of a regiment. I walked all day, and at night found myself at a small town so far from my home that I thought I might venture to stop at the inn, especially as there seemed to be no troops near. I did so. I had eaten my supper, and was about retiring, when I observed a list of deserters pasted up in one of the rooms. Hastily running it over, I saw my own description there too plainly to be mistaken. Of course, I could not remain there for the night; and, walking leisurely to the door, I was just passing out, when my attention was attracted to the conversation of two persons near.

"I am sure it must be he," said one.

"Did you read the description?—the very same hair and eyes, I am sure," said the other.

"We shall get the reward, no doubt. As soon as he has gone to bed, we will send for the officer. But come, let us go in, and take care that he does not suspect us."

As I had recognized my landlord's voice, I considered that such treachery was sufficient to justify a sudden leave; and, thinking that he might take his pay for his supper from his expected reward, I hastened away. Having travelled an hour or two, I threw myself on a pile of straw, and rested till morning, determined that I would trust myself in no one's house until I was again enlisted. It was, therefore, with pleasure that I heard, soon after sunrise, the sound of martial music in advance of me. Two hours after, I was quietly ensconced in my quarters, in the Lowth Militia, *en route* for Dublin, having the third time received my money from government.

Our progress towards the capital was very slow, as we were constantly looking out and receiving additions to our company from the peasantry of the places through which we passed. The glowing descriptions of our recruiting-sergeant, the thrilling sound of the martial music, the very sight of so many well-dressed soldiers, presented strong inducements to the ragged, half-clad, and half-starved children of poor unfortunate Ireland, to leave her shores for at least a season. Then there was the hope of returning with the pension, that would insure to them, in their old age, a sustenance, of which they could be certain from no other source.

These inducements carried desolation to many a home, but they filled our ranks; and, on the 20th of July, we were in Dublin, with complete numbers. Here I enjoyed more liberty than I had done at either of the other stations, and had more opportunity to see the place. The barracks are situated in the west end of the city, near the beautiful river which divides it into two equal parts. Not far from them rises the noble hospital of Kilmainham, destined for the reception of disabled and superannuated soldiers. The visits of these old soldiers was a source of great pleasure to us, as we were never weary of hearing them recount their tales of war and of hard-fought fields; while, in listening to our anticipations, and in seeing us go through the exercises required, they almost seemed to renew their own youth.

Orders came to Dublin for militia volunteers. Knowing that I was in as great danger, as a deserter, whilst in the militia as at home, and being proud of the opportunity of volunteering, we were called by a general order to Phoenix Park, where I volunteered from the Lowth militia into the 28th Regiment of Foot, for foreign service, and received eighteen guineas, as volunteer's pay,—being the fourth time I received the same sum.

Preparations were now rapidly being made for our departure to England; and, as the time drew near, my thoughts naturally reverted to my own dear home, and I felt it would be a great privilege if I could once more see my parents. I therefore wrote to them, giving them a full account of my wanderings, my place of destination, and begging them at least to write to me before I left, and say that I was forgiven for all the trouble and anxiety I had cost them.

The return mail brought me a letter from them, assuring me of their love and forgiveness, and promising to visit me before we left. I may as well state here that I did not see my dear parents again. They came to Dublin, as they had promised; but we had left the day before, for Cork. They would have followed me there, immediately, had they not been informed, at the barracks, that I had left directly for

England. It was the policy of our officers to prevent these meetings as often as possible, on account of their effect upon the soldiers. And no one, in whose heart lingered a particle of kindness, could look unmoved on the spectacles of misery which it was almost daily my lot to witness, when the time approached for us to leave.

Of the thousands collected there, waiting to be transferred to a foreign shore, how few would ever return! and, of those few, how many would come back, with ruined health and broken hearts, only to find desolation and death where they had hoped for love and sympathy! Many of these had enlisted while under the influence of liquor, or else had been brought in by the press-gang; and, in thus leaving their families, they were deprived of every means of subsistence, and must either soon perish from want, or linger out a more protracted, but scarcely less miserable existence, in the workhouse.

O! why must Ireland suffer so much from her poverty, with her fertile soil and many productions?—that deep poverty, which has forced so many of her sons abroad to die, and which still continues to force them abroad, to ask that assistance and aid which it were worse than useless to expect at home! Of these partings, to which I have referred, the long course of years has scarcely dimmed the painful impression they made upon my memory. One of those oftenest recalled was that of a young man who was bidding adieu to his aged parents. He was an only son, and his most diligent care and labour scarcely sufficed to supply them with the common necessaries of life. Their lease had recently expired, and to renew it again a sum of money was required which was utterly beyond their simple means. Nothing could save them from immediate ejectment unless the lease was renewed, and this faithful son determined to secure a home for his parents in their old age by gaining the bounty-money offered to volunteers. To do this, however, he must submit to a separation which he could not hope could be otherwise than final; for who would care and labour for them when he was gone? And those parents, accustomed as they had been to his presence and kindness, how could they live when the sunlight of their existence had set? Never have I seen agony more strongly depicted on the human countenance than it appeared on his, as he turned away from their farewell clasp. Poor fellow! he deserved a better fate than afterwards befell him; for he died by the hands of a guerrilla, on the hills of Spain. What became of his aged parents I never knew. We could only hope that the angel of death would be merciful, and come soon to their relief.

Turning away from this sad scene, which brought tears into eyes all unused to weep, it was only to meet another, which affected the heart almost as deeply. A woman, pale and sickly-looking, worn to premature old age by incessant toil and suffering, and the mother of five little children, was bidding farewell to her husband. He had enlisted while drunk, and had spent or lost nearly all of his money before recovering his senses. When he was able to realize his situation, his feelings could scarcely be controlled; for he was the sole dependence of his helpless family. But there was now no help for him. The money was gone, he had pledged himself, and he must go, and leave his family to starve or live on the bread of charity. But I will not dwell on this parting scene. Suffice it to say, that, when our preparations were complete, and our regiment ordered to Cork, I left Dublin, with all its magnificence, with out a regret.

We marched to Cork,—a distance of one hundred and sixty-two miles,—by slow and easy marches. I believe the regulations of the service only require ten miles' march in the course of the day; but we almost always went further than that before halting. From the time of leaving Dublin we began to receive the usual pay of an English soldier, which is one shilling per day, and two suits of clothes per year. Of this sum the government retain one half, for furnishing bread and beef. With the other sixpence the soldier is required to furnish himself with whatever else he may wish for; or, if we preferred it, while marching in Ireland, the whole sum was paid us, and then we purchased what we chose.

By being very abstemious, some of our men saved a few pence daily, which was often transmitted to the suffering ones at home. Whenever we halted for the night the soldiers were billeted upon the inhabitants of the place, each family being required to accommodate one, two, or more soldiers with lodgings and a supper.

The number of the house and the name of the street was given, on a ticket, to each soldier, which he was required to present at the door, and the family must either accommodate him, or furnish him with money to procure lodgings elsewhere. This was often very unpleasant for the inhabitants, and the alternative, of course, was frequently adopted, especially by the more wealthy classes. We were not always treated with kindness by those who were thus forced to receive us,—having frequently to put up with the poorest accommodations that could be furnished. But, as soldiers have never been noted for their forbearance or mildness, such persons usually found themselves worse off, in the end, than if they had pursued a different course.

As a general thing, when treated with kindness, it was returned with civility, especially while we were in our own country. In the wars on the continent, in the frequent passages of armies into the countries of their opponents, the inhabitants often suffered severely from this custom; and reprisals were frequently made, when opportunity offered, which, if not justified by the law of right, were most certainly by that of camps.

An incident, illustrating this, which occurred while I was

on the continent, and which afterwards appeared in the newspapers of the day, may be given here, as I shall not again have occasion to allude to this subject.

A Prussian officer, on his arrival at Paris, particularly requested to be billeted on the house of a lady, in the Faubourg St. Germain. His request was complied with, and, on his arriving at the lady's house, he was shown into a small but comfortable sitting-room, with a handsome bed-chamber adjoining it. With these rooms he appeared greatly dissatisfied, and desired that the lady should give up to her own apartment, on the first floor, which was large and elegantly furnished. To this the lady made the strongest objections; but the officer insisted, and she was under the necessity of retiring to the second floor. He afterwards sent a message to her, by one of the servants, saying that he destined the second floor for his aid-de-camp. This occasioned still stronger remonstrances from the lady, but they were totally unavailing and unattended to by the officer, whose only answer was, "Obey my orders!" He then called the cook, and informed him he must prepare a handsome dinner for six persons, and desired the lady's butler to supply the table with the best wines the cellar could afford. After dinner, he sent for his hostess. She obeyed the summons.

The officer then said to her, "No doubt, madam, you consider my conduct indecorous and brutal in the extreme."

"I must confess," she answered, "that I did not expect such treatment from an officer; as, in general, military men are ever disposed to show a great degree of respect and deference to our sex."

"You think me, then, a most perfect barbarian? Answer me, frankly."

"If you really desire my undisguised opinion on the subject," said the lady, "I must say that I think your conduct truly barbarous."

"Madam," was the answer, "I am entirely of your opinion; but I only wished to give you a specimen of the behaviour and conduct of your son, during *six months* that he resided in my house, after the entrance of the French army into the Prussian capital. I do not intend, however, to follow so bad an example. You have full liberty, therefore, to resume your apartment to-morrow, and I will seek lodgings at some public hotel." The lady retired, quite satisfied that the officer was, after all, an honourable man.

While passing through a small village, not far from Cork, it was my fortune to be billeted, with two of my comrades, in a house where the eldest daughter was that evening to be married. The company had already assembled, when, knocking at the door, we presented our billets. The master of the house came to meet his unwelcome guests. He offered us quite a large sum to seek some other place for the night; but, as we had obtained an inkling of what was going forward, we declined. Of course, no alternative remained but to receive us with as good a grace as he could. I am happy to say, however, that we did not forget what was due to our hosts, in the way of decorum, although we joined in the merry dance, and saluted the bride with soldier-like freedom. Money was often made by the soldiers, when they chose to do so, as they would frequently receive three, five, or even ten shillings, for their tickets, and then furnish themselves with cheaper lodgings elsewhere.

We arrived in Cork in September. This large city is next in size to Dublin, and lies one hundred and sixty-two miles to the south-west of it. It was originally built upon an island, but in process of time it was extended to both sides of the river. Its harbour is nine miles from the city. It is a beautiful, harbour, very safe and capacious. Here we remained until the middle of October, when we were ordered to sail for England. The transport *Lunar* was sent to convey us, and, having received her complement of men, she was soon under way. Almost all on board were new recruits, who were leaving Ireland for the first time, and it was with various and deep emotions that we watched her fast-receding shores. Mingled with many sad recollections of parents, and home, and friends, came dreams of future glory, the thirst for martial fame, and anticipations of the happiness we should enjoy in scenes far away, whose very distance and indistinctness added, far more than exact reality could have done, to the brightness of our hopes.

But, however golden might have been the visions that filled our minds, we were certainly destined to realize none of them on that day. Sea-sickness soon sent us all to our berths, and a more miserable, woebegone looking set than our company presented could not easily be found. But though none of *us* felt inclined to laugh, a looker-on might have found much amusement, in the grotesque attitudes, the comical grimaces, and the unavailing complaints, that resounded on every side. But, however much the old tars on board might have been disposed to make themselves merry at our expense, the next day gave them sufficient occupation in attending to their own affairs.

The morning that we left the beautiful harbour of Cork was fair and cloudless. The gentle breeze, directly in our favour, carried us out into the channel with an easy, gliding motion, that promised us a short and pleasant voyage. But when, just at night, weary of the confinement and confusion in our cabin, I crept on deck, I saw the captain and mate conversing in low and hurried accents, while the sailors were watching the dark, portentous clouds, that lay piled up against the horizon, gilded by the last rays of the sun, which made their darkness seem still blacker.

The wind, which had been directly in our favour, now tacked to the opposite quarter, and was blowing with great fury, which increased before midnight to a perfect hurricane. Our vessel, with its closely-reefed sails, flew over the mountain waves, like a bird before the storm. For two days and two nights the storm continued, and our vessel seemed as a mere plaything of the waves.

On the third morning it became almost unmanageable, and we had little hope of reaching land in safety; but, as we came in sight of the white cliffs of England, the storm subsided, and our hopes again rose. Our captain tried hard to reach our point of destination, but all his efforts were fruitless, as the ship was almost a wreck. Giving up this point, therefore, he succeeded in reaching the little port of Pill, about four miles from Bristol, where we landed in safety. I shall never forget the emotion of joy which thrilled my heart when I found myself once more on land; and I presume there were none on board who did not, in some degree, share the feeling.

From Pill we proceeded to Bristol, where we remained a short time. We enjoyed our stay in Bristol very much, as there were many things that were new to us to attract our attention, and we were not as closely watched as we had been in Ireland. Our pay, while in England, was one and sixpence daily,—the amount being increased, as provisions were dearer than in Ireland.

From Bristol we were ordered to Plymouth, to undergo the necessary but wearisome task of being drilled,—a task not much more agreeable to our officers than to ourselves. It would have indeed required the patience of a Job to mould those raw recruits, unaccustomed to confinement, and totally unused to that subordination so positively necessary in an army, into skilful and obedient soldiers. It was, indeed, a tiresome task; and it was with no small degree of pleasure that we learned that our time had expired, and that we were soon to embark for the Peninsula.

The day at length arrived when we were actually to sail. The last preparations had been made,—the last stores taken in. Each ship (there were eleven in the whole) received its living load, and then, one after another, their white sails were spread, and soon the fast-receding shores of England seemed but a dim line, and then a mere speck on the horizon. It was on the first day of January, 1811, that we bade our long, and so many of us our last farewell, to the shores of old England.

On our own ship there were twelve hundred of us,—a jovial, merry set. For the first fourteen days nothing worthy of special notice occurred, but then an accident happened which came near costing us all our lives. It is the custom, on board ships-of-war, to serve out every day spirit rations to the men. On our ship, this was done at eleven o'clock in the morning. A cask of liquor was rolled on deck, the head knocked out, and the officer whose duty it was served out to each of the mess a measure of raw spirit. They usually came up, one by one, received their measure, and then retired, either to drink it themselves or to dispose of it to others, who could always be found willing to purchase, which was often done, when any of us had more than usual need of money.

On the morning to which I have alluded, the 14th of January, one of the soldiers walked up to the cask for his allowance with a lighted pipe in his mouth, the coal from which he dropped accidentally in the liquor. Almost in a moment the whole deck was enveloped in flames. The alarm was soon given, and every man on board did his utmost to extinguish them; but the large quantity of tar and other combustibles made this a task not easily accomplished. The deck was soon flooded with water, but the flames leaped up the ropes, and caught on the rigging. In spite of all our efforts, they still gained ground, and so rapidly that the most daring of our number began to fear that we were lost. As a last resource, each of the soldiers caught their blankets, and throwing them wet on the fire, and keeping them so, it was at length extinguished. When this was completed, we gathered the remains of our charred and ruined blankets, and, throwing them into the sea, we retired to our naked berths, grateful that, though suffering with cold, our lives had been spared.

It has often been my lot, in the crowded city, to witness the raging flames, as they leaped from house to house, carrying ruin and desolation in their progress; I have gazed on the ashes of palaces, beautiful but yesterday in their magnificence, to which the ruthless torch of the midnight incendiary had been applied; and I have often, often been startled from the deep sleep of night, by that fearful cry, which, in its very name, is the token of suffering and sorrow;—but never—never do I remember anything that thrilled to the depths of my soul like that cry of fire, on the wild waste of waters, where, unless it could be subdued, scarcely a hope remained for the safety of those twelve hundred human beings, confined in the ship's narrow space.

On land, there must be at least a hope of escape; and then we know that the warm sympathies of active friends are enlisted in the sufferers' behalf, and that all that man can do, to aid or save, will be done. But when, far away on the sea, the red flames are seen leaping from mast to mast, no summoning bell tolls out its warning voice on the midnight air,—no friendly crowds rush to the rescue; but the little band of devoted ones on board must toil and labour, with all that energy which the human spirit will summon up when life or death hang on the passing moment, until the die is cast. Then, if all is at last in vain, it but remains to choose a death by fire or flood, or, too often, in the few that may escape by the boats, a more lingering, but not less to be dreaded fate, is met in death by starvation. But such was not our destiny; and among all the narrow escapes which it has been my lot in life to encounter, there are no deliverances I remember with more gratitude than the quenching of that fire on board our man-of-war.

In referring to this incident of my life, I have often wondered that a custom so full of danger as that of serving spirit out daily to such a body of men should be continued. The frequent accidents to which I allude are but a very small part of the evil; yet even this is well worthy of being taken into consideration, when we remember not only the pecuniary loss involved, but the vast amount of human life which is thus needlessly sacrificed. The moral evil is of far greater magnitude.

When I left home, I had never formed the habit of drinking,—the taste of liquor was positively disagreeable to me; and it was in compliance with this custom that I first found a relish for it. I can recall many, who now fill a drunkard's grave, who might trace back the commencement of this sinful and ruinous habit to the same practice. It is my humble opinion that much of the disobedience and disrespectful language from the men might be avoided, and consequently many of the punishments dispensed with, if this custom were wholly discontinued. Besides, is it not encouraging this ruinous habit, thus to place, as it were, the national seal upon its usefulness and necessity, by thus furnishing it to those employed, and especially just before a battle? as if *that* were in any way necessary to infuse a true spirit of courage! It is much to be hoped that a decided reform will soon be effected here; and that, while philanthropists are striving with such earnestness to do away with much of the corporal punishment formerly in vogue in both army and navy, they will not forget the exciting cause which so often operates to destroy entirely the force of moral restraint, thus rendering physical coercion not only advisable, but often absolutely necessary.

While passing through the Bay of Biscay, we encountered a terrific storm, which entirely scattered our little fleet. Most of the time, since leaving home, we had remained within hailing distance of each other, messages often passing and repassing; but when the storm burst upon us with so much fury, the rest of the ships were quickly driven away. Only one vessel remained in sight. It was the smallest of our fleet, and we watched it with much anxiety, as we could plainly see that it had undergone serious injury. It was on the evening of the second day that we heard the distant booming of her guns, through the wild roar of the waters, announcing their perilous situation, and imploring, if possible, aid. But what could human arm avail, in a time like this? Our own ship lay at the mercy of the waves. No boat could live for one moment in those foaming and raging waters; and so, with aching hearts, we were compelled to look idly on, and see our countrymen and fellow-soldiers about to be engulfed in a watery grave.

Night closed in; we could see that their condition was hopeless; and, before nine, their last light was extinguished, nor did we ever hear from them again. In all probability, the whole crew of six hundred men were lost.

The next morning the sun rose bright and beautiful, and the moaning waves lashed themselves to rest as peacefully as though their bright waters hid no dark secrets, to be veiled from human view until the sea shall give up its dead. The wind passed into a favourable quarter, and the gentle breeze soon wafted us on, until the high lands of Spain rose full on our view.

Accustomed to the level shores of Ireland, I had never im-agined scenery so beautiful as that which appeared all along the coast, presenting a view said to be the finest in the world. Our fleet, slowly collecting together, now rounded the cape, and we soon found ourselves in the Bay of Gibraltar. This bay is eight miles long, and five wide. Every eye was on the alert for the first view of that great rock, so deservedly famous in English history; and we soon saw it, rising, as it does, fifteen hundred feet out of the sea, and extending over three miles. It is one of the strongest fortifications in the world. It is owned by the British government.

As our fleet dropped their anchors in this noble harbour, we were welcomed at the fort by martial salutes and loud huzzas, which were heartily returned. It was with much pleasure that we found ourselves at last in that land of which we had heard so much, and where we hoped to witness, and participate in, many deeds of glory. After marching, with flying colours and beating drums, into the town, we were at liberty to go where we pleased; and I soon found myself, with a party of my countrymen, on the famous rock. Rising perpendicularly out of the sea, it slopes towards the shore, and is level for a few feet on the top. On this level space are placed the cannon, which command the whole entrance into the Mediterranean. The dim outline of the African shore is distinctly visible from its top.

We were much annoyed by the monkeys, that inhabit the rock in great numbers. They are said to come over from Africa, by a subterranean passage, under the Straits. They were regarded almost as sacred by the inhabitants, and a fine is imposed on any one who injures or kills them. They sometimes attack their assailants with stones, but oftener prefer stratagem to valour,—running rapidly before their pursuers until, by a sudden turn on some dizzy edge, they secure themselves, and leave their pursuers to be dashed to pieces on the rocks. They are often quite troublesome to the soldiers and sentries, pelting them with stones, and always ready to retaliate.

Gibraltar is called the key of the Mediterranean, because no force could possibly effect an entrance without permission from the British government. They have now mounted there over eight hundred guns, and are intending to increase the number to one thousand. The English territory in the south of Spain is about four miles in extent. They obtained possession of it only after severe struggles; but can probably never be dispossessed by open force.

The Sabbath after we landed, the whole company of men were paraded for church. We were all ordered to attend the service of the Church of England. As I had been brought up a strict Catholic, and as there was a church of that persuasion in the place, to which I intended going, I did not respond to the call, but remained in my quarters. I had been here but a short time, when the sergeant came in, and asked why I did not go to church. I told him I could not attend the service of his church while there was one of my own denomination in the place. He replied that it was a rule of the army, and I must submit to it. But I still declined to go, when he went out and reported to the adjutant that I had refused to obey orders. The adjutant then came in, and asked me the same question. I told him that I was not a member of the Church of England, but a Catholic. If I could be permitted, I would gladly attend my own church, but could not be present at the service.

At this the adjutant was very angry, and ordered me into confinement. Here I had leisure to reflect on the probable consequences of the step I had taken. Punishment of some kind was certain; and, judging from the angry appearance and words of the adjutant, I certainly had no reason to think it would be a light one. But what right has England, I asked myself, to compel those who fight her battles to worship as she worships? My conscience told me that she had none. I felt that my cause was just, and I determined to persevere, whatever might be the result.

The next day I was summoned before a court-martial, tried, and sentenced to receive three hundred lashes on the succeeding day. As, perhaps, some of my young readers have not much idea of this punishment, I will describe it to them.

A triangle was erected, composed of three poles, fastened at the top with an iron bolt. To two of these the legs and hands of the sufferer are designed to be fastened, while a board is placed across for the breast to lean upon. The troops were then marched out, and formed a large hollow square around the place of punishment. I was then brought to the place, under guard of a file of soldiers, commanded by an officer. My clothes were so far removed as to leave me naked to the waist, and I was bound to the triangle. Turning to the first soldier on the file, the officer directed that he should proceed to duty. He laid aside his coat, and applied twenty-five lashes, with the cat-o'-nine-tails, to my back. These blows were counted by the officer.

After twenty-five had been applied, I was asked if I would give up; I answered, "No!" The blood was already flowing freely from my back, yet I resolved to die rather than submit to what appeared to me so unjust a requirement. The next soldier then took the lash, and struck twenty-five times. Again the officer asked if I would yield, and received the same reply; and this Was continued until the whole three hundred had been inflicted. I was then taken down, more dead than alive, and sent to the hospital to be cured of my wounds,—a process usually requiring from six weeks to three months. The cat—the instrument with which this punishment is inflicted—is composed of nine small cords, twisted very hard, and having three knots on each cord; sometimes the ends of these are bound with wire. The whip is usually about eighteen inches long, and the handle fifteen.

As soon as I was able, I wrote to his Royal Highness the Duke of York, stating my case, and requesting permission for those who preferred attending their own churches to do so. I was much gratified to learn that his Highness took the matter into consideration; and, soon after, sent an order that the soldiers should be permitted to attend church where they pleased. I have always had the consolation, when looking back on that scene of severe and unjust suffering, of thinking that it was instrumental in procuring liberty of conscience to many who might never have enjoyed it without.

I remained at the hospital until our troops were ordered to march, which was only three or four weeks.

Of course, the wounds were only partially healed, and I was obliged to shoulder my knapsack while they were still raw and sore. This constant irritation prevented their healing, and the suffering I endured from this cause I considered nearly as great as that from the punishment itself.

CHAPTER 2

War in the Peninsula

Before entering into a particular account of the battles in which I was myself an actor, it might not be uninteresting to my readers to take a hasty survey of the war which was now raging in the Peninsula, and the causes which led to British intervention. In doing this, I can, of course, in so small a work, only allude to its principal events, and relate some anecdotes, interesting, as well from their authenticity, as from the patriotism of which they were such bright examples.

Charles IV., a descendant of the Spanish Bourbons, in 1807, occupied the throne of Spain. He was feeble in mind, impotent in action, and extremely dissolute in his habits. Writing to Napoleon, he gives an account of himself which must have filled with contempt the mind of the hard-working emperor for the imbecile king who thus- disgraced a throne:

> Every day, winter as well as summer, I go out to shoot, from morning till noon. I then dine, and return to the chase, which I continue till sunset. Manuel Godoy then gives me a brief account of what is going on, and I go to bed, to recommence the same life on the morrow.

His wife, Louisa, was a shameless profligate. She had selected, from the body-guard of the king, a young soldier, named Godoy, as her principal favourite; and had freely lavished on him both wealth and honours. He was known as the Prince of Peace. A favourite of the king, as well as queen, the realm was, in reality, governed by him. Ferdinand, Prince of the Asturias, and heir to the throne, hated this favourite. Weak, unprincipled, and ambitious, unwilling to wait until the crown should become his by inheritance, it is said that he concerted a scheme to remove both his parents by poison. He was arrested, and imprisoned. Natural affection was entirely extinct in the bosoms of his parents. Louisa, speaking of her son, said that "he had a mule's head and a tiger's heart;" and history informs us that if injustice is done here, it is only to the tiger and mule.

Both king and queen did all they could to cover his name with obloquy, and prepare the nation for his execution. But the popular voice was with Ferdinand. The rule of the base-born favourite could not be tolerated by the Spanish *hidalgos*; and the nation, groaning under the burdens that the. vices and misrule of Charles had brought upon them, looked with hope to the youth, whose very abandonment had excited an interest in his favour. From the depths of his prison he wrote to Napoleon, imploring his aid, and requesting an alliance with his family. Charles, too, invoked the assistance "of the hero destined by Providence to save Europe and support thrones."

A secret treaty was concluded between the emperor and Charles, whose object was nominally the conquest of Portugal; and thus French troops were brought to Madrid. A judicial investigation was held on the charge against Ferdinand, which ended in the submission of that prince to his parents. But the intrigues of the two parties still continued. In March, 1808, hatred of. Godoy, and contempt of the king, had increased to such a degree, that the populace of Madrid could no longer be controlled.

The palace of the Prince of Peace was broken open and sacked. The miserable favourite, allowed scarcely a moment's warning of the coming storm, had barely time to conceal himself beneath a pile of old mats, in his garret. Here, for thirty-six hours, he lay, shivering with terror and suffering. Unable longer to endure the pangs of thirst, he crept down from his hiding-place, was seen, and dragged out by the mob. A few select troops of the king rushed to his rescue; and, half dead with fright and bruises, he was thrown into prison.

The populace, enraged by the loss of their victim, now threatened to attack the palace. Charles, alarmed for his own safety, abdicated in favour of Ferdinand, and that prince was proclaimed king, amid the greatest rejoicings. But Charles wrote to Napoleon that his abdication was a forced one, and again implored his aid. Soon after, determined to advocate his cause in person, he went to Bayonne to meet the emperor, accompanied by Louisa and Godoy, and, with them, his two younger sons. Ferdinand, jealous of his father's influence with Napoleon, determined to confront him there.

His people everywhere declared against this measure. They cut the traces of his carriage; they threw themselves before the horses, imploring him, with prayers and tears, not to desert his people. But Ferdinand went on. The emperor received them all with kindness. In a private interview with him, Charles, Louisa, and Godoy, willingly exchanged their rights to the uneasy crown of Spain for a luxurious home in Italy, where money for the gratification of all their voluptuous desires should be at their command.

Ferdinand and his two brothers, Carlos and Francisco, were not so easily persuaded to surrender the crown of their ancestors. But Napoleon's iron will at length prevailed, and the three brothers remained not unwilling prisoners in the castle of Valencey. The throne of Spain was now vacant. The right to fill it was assumed by the emperor, in virtue of the cession to him, by Charles, of his rights. The council of Castile, the municipality of Madrid, and the governing junta, in obedience to Napoleon's dictate, declared that their choice had fallen upon Joseph Bonaparte, King of Naples. He was already on his way to Bayonne. On the 20th of July he entered Madrid; and, on the 24th, he was proclaimed King of Spain and the Indies. But, if the rulers of Spain, and a few of her pusillanimous nobles, had agreed to accept a king of Napoleon's choice, not so decided the great body of the people. They everywhere flew to arms.

To acknowledge the authority of the self-constituted government, was to declare one's self an enemy to the nation. Assassinations at Cadiz and Seville were imitated in every part of Spain. Grenada had its murders; Carthagena rivalled Cadiz in ruthless cruelty; and Valencia reeked with blood. In Gallicia, the people assembled and endeavoured to oblige their governor to declare war against France. Prompted by prudence, he advised them to delay. Enraged at this, the ferocious soldiers seized him, and, planting their weapons in the earth, tossed him on their points, and left him to die. In Asturias, two noblemen were selected, and sent to implore the assistance of England. In England, the greatest enthusiasm prevailed.

The universal rising of the Spanish nation was regarded as a pledge of their patriotism, and aid and assistance was immediately promised and given. Napoleon, with his usual promptness, poured his troops into Spain. They were successful in many places; but the enemy, always forming in small numbers, if easily defeated, soon appeared in another place.

The first permanent stand was made at Saragossa. Palafox had, with some hastily gathered followers, disputed the passage of the Ebro, and, routed by superior force, had fallen back upon this city, whose heroic defence presents acts of daring courage of which the world's history scarcely furnishes a parallel. It was regularly invested by the French, under Lefebre Desnouttes. The city had no regular defences, but the houses were very strong, being vaulted so as to be nearly fire-proof, and the massy walls of the convents afforded security to the riflemen who filled them. The French troops had at one time nearly gained possession of the town, but, for some unknown reasons, they fell back. This gave confidence to the besieged. They redoubled their exertions. All shared the labour,—women, children, priests and friars, laboured for the common cause,—and in twenty-four hours the defences were so strengthened that the place was prepared to stand a siege.

But the next morning Palafox imprudently left the city, and offered battle to the French. He was, of course, quickly beaten; but succeeded in escaping, with a few of his troops, into the city. A small hill rises close to the convent of St. Joseph's, called Monte Torrero. Some stone houses on this hill were strongly fortified, and occupied by twelve hundred men. This place was attacked by Lefebre, and taken by assault, on the 27th of June, 1808. The convents of St. Joseph's and the Capuchins were next attacked by the French, and, after a long resistance, taken by storm.

The command of the besiegers was now transferred to General Verdier. He continued the siege during the whole of July, making several assaults on the gates, from which he was repulsed, with great loss. The Spaniards, having received a reinforcement, made a sortie to retake Monte Torrero; but were defeated, their commander killed, and most of their number left dead.

On the 2nd of August, the enemy opened a dreadful fire on the town. One of their shells lighted upon the powder magazine, which was in the most secure part of the city, and blew it up, destroying many houses and killing numbers of the besieged. The carnage, during this siege, was truly terrible. Six hundred women and children perished, and above forty thousand men were killed.

It was at this place that the act of female heroism so beautifully celebrated by Byron was performed. An assault had been
made upon one of the gates, which was withstood with great
courage by the besieged. At the battery of the Portillo, their
fire had been so fatal, that but one artillery-man remained able
to serve the gun. He seemed to bear a charmed life. Though
shot and shell fell thick and fast around him, he still stood unharmed, and rapidly loaded and discharged his gun.

At length, worn out by his own exertions, his strength
seemed about to fail. There was little time, in a contest like
this, to watch for the safety of others; but there was one eye
near which not for a moment lost sight of him. Augustina, a
girl twenty-two years of age, had followed her daring lover
to his post. She would not leave him there alone, although
every moment exposed her to share his death. When she saw
his strength begin to fail, she seized a cordial, and held it to
his lips. In the very act of receiving it, the fatal death-stroke
came, and he fell dead at her feet.

Not for a moment paused the daring maid. No tear fell
for the slain. She lived to do what he had done. Snatching a
match from the hand of a dead artillery-man, she fired off the
gun, and swore never to quit it alive, during the siege. The
soldiers and citizens, who had begun to retire, stimulated by
so heroic an example, rushed to the battery a second time,
and again opened a tremendous fire upon the enemy. For
this daring act, Augustina received a small shield of honour,
and had the word "Saragossa" embroidered on the sleeve of
her dress, with the pay of an artillery-man. Byron thus com-
memorates this heroism, in his own transcendent manner:

The Spanish maid, aroused,
Hangs on the willow her unstrung guitar,
And, all unsexed, the anlace hath espoused,
Sung the loud song, and dared the deeds of war.

And she, whom once the semblance of a scar
Appalled, an owlet's 'larum filled with dread,
Now views the column-scattering bayonet jar,
The falchion flash, and o'er the yet warm dead
Stalks with Minerva's step, where Mars might quake to tread.

Ye who shall marvel when you hear her tale,
O! had you known her in the softer hour,—
Marked her black eye, that mocks her coal-black veil,—
Heard her light, lively tones in lady's bower,—
Seen her long locks, that foil the painter's power,—
Her fairy form, with more than female grace,—
Scarce would you deem that Saragossa's tower
Beheld her smile in danger's Gorgon face,
Thin the closed ranks, and lead in glory's fearful chase!

Her lover sinks—she sheds no ill-timed tear;
Her chief is slain—she fills his fatal post;
Her fellows flee—she checks their base career;
The foe retires—she heads the sallying host,
Who can appease like her a lover's ghost?
Who can avenge so well a leader's fall?
What maid retrieve, when man's flushed hope is lost?
Who hang so fiercely on the flying Gaul,
Foiled by a woman's hand, before the battered wall!

On the 4th of August, the French stormed the city, and
penetrated as far as the Corso, or public square. Here a terrible conflict was maintained. Every inch of ground was
manfully contested; but the enemy's cavalry was irresistible,
and the besieged began to give way. All appeared lost. The
French, thinking the victory gained, began to plunder. Seeing this, the besieged rallied, and attacked them. They succeeded in driving the enemy back to the Corso. They also
set fire to the convent of Francisco, and many perished in its
conflagration.

Night now came, to add its horrors to the scene. The fierce contest still raged on. The lunatic asylum was invaded, and soon the dread cry of "Fire" mingled with the incoherent ravings of its inmates.

"Here," says one writer, "were to be seen grinning maniacs, shouting with hideous joy, and mocking the cries of the wounded; there, others, with seeming delight, were dabbling in the crimson fluid of many a brave heart, which had scarcely ceased to beat. On one side, young and lovely women, dressed in the fantastic rigging of a mind diseased, were bearing away headless trunks and mutilated limbs, which lay scattered around them, while the unearthly cries of the idiot kept up a hideous concert with the shouts of the infuriated combatants. In short, it was a scene of unmingled horror, too fearful for the mind to dwell upon."

After a severe contest and dreadful carnage, the French forced their way into the Corso, in the very centre of the city, and before night were in possession of one-half of it. Lefebre now believed that he had effected his purpose, and required Palafox to surrender, in a note containing only these words: "Headquarters, St. Engracia,—Capitulation." Equally laconic the brave Spaniard's answer was: "Headquarters, Saragossa,—War to the knife's point."

The contest which was now carried on stands unparalleled. One side of the Corso was held by the French soldiery; the opposite was in possession of the Arragonese, who erected batteries at the end of the cross-streets, within a few paces of those the French had thrown up. The space between these was covered with the dead. Next day, the powder of the besieged began to fail; but even this dismayed them not.

One cry broke from the people, whenever Palafox came among them, "War to the knife!—no capitulation." The night was coming on, and still the French continued their impetuous onsets. But now the brother of Palafox entered the city with a convoy of arms and ammunition, and a reinforcement of three thousand men. This succour was as unexpected as it was welcome, and raised the desperate courage of the citizens to the highest pitch of enthusiasm.

The war was now carried on from street to street, and even from room to room. A priest, by the name of Santiago Suss, displayed the, most undaunted bravery, fighting at the head of the besieged, and cheering and consoling the wounded and the dying. At the head of forty chosen men, he succeeded in procuring a supply of powder for the town, and, by united stratagem and courage, effected its entrance, even through the French lines.

This murderous contest was continued for eleven successive days and nights,—more, indeed, by night than by day, for it was almost certain death to appear by daylight within reach of houses occupied by the other party. But, concealed by the darkness of the night, they frequently dashed across the street, to attack each other's batteries; and the battle, commenced there, was often carried into the houses beyond, from room to room, and from floor to floor.

As if not enough of suffering had accompanied this memorable siege, a new scourge came to add its horrors to the scene. Pestilence, with all its accumulated terrors, burst upon the doomed city. Numbers of putrescent bodies, in various stages of decomposition, were strewed thickly around the spot where the death-struggle was still going on. The air was impregnated with the pestiferous miasm of festering mortality; and this, too, in a climate like Spain, and in the month of August! This evil must be removed,—but how? Certain death would have been the penalty of any Arragonese who should attempt it.

The only remedy was to tie ropes to the French prisoners, and, pushing them forward amid the dead and dying, compel them to remove the bodies, and bring them away for interment. Even for this office, as necessary to one party as the other, there was no truce; only the prisoners were better secured, by the compassion of their countrymen, from the fire.

From day to day, this heroic defence was kept up, with unremitting obstinacy. In vain breaches were made and stormed; the besiegers were constantly repulsed. At last Verdier received orders to retire; and the French, after reducing the city almost to ashes, were compelled to abandon their attacks, and retreat.

Meanwhile, all over Spain the contest was continued, and everywhere with the most unsparing cruelty. Her purest and noblest sons often fell victims to private malice. "No one's life," says one author, "was worth a week's purchase." One anecdote may serve as an example to illustrate the spirit of the times.

It was night. The rays of the full moon shed their beautiful light on the hills of the Sierra Morena. On one of these hills lay a small division of the patriotic army. Its chief was a dark, fierce-looking man, in whose bosom the spirit of human kindness seemed extinct forever. A brigand, who had long dealt in deeds of death, he had placed himself without the pale even of the laws of Spain. But, when the war commenced, he had offered his own services and that of his men against the French, and had been accepted.

On this night he sat, wrapped in his huge cloak, beside the decaying watch-fire, seemingly deep in thought. Near him lay a prisoner on the grass, with the knotted cords so firmly hound around his limbs that the black blood seemed every moment ready to burst from its enclosure. He might have groaned aloud in his agony, had not the pride of his nation,—for he, too, was a Spaniard,—and his own deep courage, prevented. His crime was, that, yielding to the promptings of humanity, he had shown kindness to a wounded French officer, and had thus drawn upon himself suspicion of favouring their cause. Short trial was needed, in those days, to doom a man to death; and, with the morning's dawn, the brave Murillo was informed that he must die.

With closed eyes and a calm countenance, his heart was yet filled with agony, as he remembered his desolated home and his defenceless little ones. Suddenly, a light footstep was heard in the wood adjoining.

The sentinel sprang to his feet, and demanded, "Who goes there? "A boy, over whose youthful brow scarce twelve summers could have passed, answered the summons.

"I would speak with your chief," he said. The ruthless man raised his head as the boy spoke this; and, not waiting for an answer, he sprang forward and stood before him.

"What is your errand here, boy?" asked the brigand.

"I come a suppliant for my father's life," he said, pointing to the prisoner on the grass.

"He dies with the morrow's sun," was the unmoved reply.

"Nay, chieftain, spare him, for my mother's sake, and for her children. Let *him* live, and, if you must have blood, I will die for him;" and the noble boy threw himself at the feet of the chief, and looked up imploringly in his face. "He is so good!—You smile: you will save his life!"

"You speak lightly of life," said the stern man, "and you know little of death. Are you willing to lose one of your ears, for your father's sake?"

"I am," said the boy, and he removed his cap, and fixed his eyes on his father's face. Not a single tear fell, as the severed member, struck off by the chief's hand, lay at his feet.

"You bear it bravely, boy; are you willing to lose the other?"

"If it will save my father's life," was the unfaltering response. A moment more, and the second one lay beside its fellow, while yet not a groan, or word expressive of suffering, passed the lips of the noble child. "Will you now release my father?" he asked, as he turned to the prostrate man, whose tears, which his own pain had no power to bring forth, fell thick and fast, as he witnessed the bravery of his unoffending son. For a moment it seemed that a feeling of compassion had penetrated the flinty soul of the man of blood. But, if the spark had fallen, it glimmered but a moment on the cold iron of that heart, and then went out forever.

"Before I release him, tell me who taught you thus to endure suffering."

"My father," answered the boy.

"Then that father must die; for Spain is not safe while he lives to rear such children." And before the morning dawned father and son slept their last sleep.

While Lefebre and Verdier were prosecuting the fatal siege of Saragossa, Marshal Bessieres was pursuing his victorious course in Castile, compelling one force after another to acknowledge the authority of Joseph. General Duhesme and Marshal Moncey, in Catalonia, met with varied success;—repulsed at Valencia and at Gerona, they yet met with enough good fortune to maintain their reputation as generate. In Andalusia, the French army, under Dupont, met with serious reverses.

At Baylen, eighteen thousand men laid down their arms, only stipulating that they should be sent to France. This capitulation, disgraceful in itself to the French, was shamefully broken. Eighty of the officers were murdered, at Lebrixa, in cold blood; armed only with their swords, they kept their assassins some time at bay, and succeeded in retreating into an open space in the town, where they endeavoured to defend themselves; but, a fire being opened upon them from the surrounding houses, the last of these unfortunate men were destroyed.

The rest of the troops were marched to Cadiz, and many died on the road. Those who survived the march were treated with the greatest indignity, and cast into the hulks, at that port. Two years afterwards, a few hundreds of them escaped, by cutting the cables of their prison-ship, and drifting in a storm upon a lee shore. The remainder were sent to the desert island of Cabrera, without clothing, without provisions, with scarcely any water, and there died by hundreds. It is related that some of them dug several feet into the solid stone with a single knife, in search of water. They had no shelter, nor was there any means of providing it. At the close of the war, when returning peace caused an exchange of prisoners, only a few hundred of all those thousands remained alive.

This victory at Baylen greatly encouraged the Spanish troops, whose ardour was beginning to fail, before the conquering career of Bessieres, and the disgust and terror occasioned by the murders and excesses of the populace. When the news of the capitulation reached Madrid, Joseph called a council of war, and it was decided that the French should abandon Madrid, and retire behind the Ebro.

But if the French arms had met with a reverse in Spain, it was compensated by their success in Portugal. Junot, at the head of twenty-five thousand men, marched from Alcantara to Lisbon. At an unfavourable season of the year, and encountering fatigue, and want, and tempests, that daily thinned his ranks, until of his whole force only two thousand remained, he yet entered Lisbon victorious. This city contained three hundred thousand inhabitants, and fourteen thousand regular troops were collected there.

A powerful British fleet was at the mouth of the harbour, and its commander, Sir Sidney Smith, offered his powerful aid, in resisting the French; yet such was the terror that Napoleon's name excited, and such the hatred of their rulers, that the people of Lisbon yielded, almost without a struggle. When Napoleon, in his *Moniteur*, made the startling announcement that "the house of Braganza had ceased to reign," the feeble prince-regent, alarmed for his own safety, embarked, with his whole court, and sailed for the Brazils. Junot himself was created Duke of Abrantes, and made governor-general of the kingdom. He exerted himself to give an efficient government to Portugal; and met with such success, that a strong French interest was created, and steps were actually taken to have Prince Eugene declared King of Portugal.

The people themselves, and the literary men, were in favour of this step; but it met with the strongest opposition from the priests, and this was nurtured and fanned into a flame by persons in the pay of the English, whose whole influence was exerted in making Napoleon's name and nation as odious to the people as possible.

Among a people so superstitious as the Portuguese, the monks would, of course, exert great influence; and many were the prodigies which appeared, to prove that their cause was under the protection of Heaven. Among others, was that of an *egg,* marked by some chemical process, with certain letters, which were interpreted to indicate the coming of Don Sebastian, King of Portugal. This adventurous monarch, years before, earnestly desirous of promoting the interests of his country, and of the Christian religion, had raised a large army, consisting of the flower of his nobility, and the choicest troops of his kingdom, and crossed the Straits into Africa, for the purpose of waging war with the Moorish king. Young, ardent and inexperienced, he violated every dictate of prudence, by marching into the enemy's country to meet an army compared with which his own was a mere handful.

The whole of his army perished, and his own fate was never known. But, as his body was not found among the dead, the peasantry of Portugal, ardently attached to their king, believed that he would some time return, and deliver his country from all their woes. He was supposed to be concealed in a secret island, waiting the destined period, in immortal youth. The prophecy of the *egg* was, therefore, believed; and people, even of the higher classes, were often seen on the highest points of the hills, looking towards the sea with earnest gaze, for the appearance of the island where their long-lost hero was detained.

The constant efforts of the English and the priests at length had their effect, in arousing the Portuguese peasantry into action; and the news of the insurrection in Spain added new fuel to the flame. The Spaniards in Portugal immediately rose against the French; and their situation would have become dangerous in the extreme, had not the promptness and dexterity of Junot succeeded in averting the danger for the present. Such was the state of affairs in the Peninsula, when the English troops made their descent into Spain. It has often been said that England was moved by pure patriotism, or by a strong desire to relieve the Spanish nation, in being thus prodigal of her soldiers and treasures; but her hatred to Napoleon, and her determination, at all hazards, to put a stop to his growing power, was, in all probability, the real motive that influenced her to bestow aid upon that people.

The English collected their army of nine thousand in Cork, in June, 1808. Sir Hugh Dalrymple had, nominally the chief command of the army, and Sir Harry Burrard the second; but the really acting officers were, Sir Arthur Wellesley and Sir John Moore. These troops disembarked at the Mondego river on the first of August, and marching along the coast, proceeded to Rolica, where they determined to give battle to the French. Junot, having left in Lisbon a sufficient force to hold the revolutionary movement in check, placed himself at the head of his army, and advanced to the contest. He was not, however, present at the battle of Rolico.

The French troops were under the command of Generals Loison and Laborde. Nearly in the centre of the heights of Rolica stands an old Moorish castle. This, and every favourable post on the high ground, was occupied by detachments of the French army. It was a strong position; but Sir Arthur, anxious to give battle before the two divisions of the French army should effect a junction, decided upon an immediate attack.

It was morning, and a calm and quiet beauty seemed to linger on the scene of the impending conflict. The heights of Rolica, though steep and difficult of access, possess few of the sterner and more imposing features of mountain scenery. The heat of summer had deprived them of much of that brightness of verdure common in a colder climate. Here and there the face of the heights was indented by deep ravines, worn by the winter torrents, the precipitous banks of which were occasionally covered with wood, and below extended groves of the cork tree and olive; while Obidas, with its ancient walls and fortress, and stupendous aqueduct, rose in the middle distance. In the east Mount Junto reared its lofty summit, while on the west lay the broad Atlantic. And this was the battle-ground that was to witness the first outpouring of that blood which flowed so profusely, on both sides, during the progress of this long and desolating war.

Sir Arthur had divided his army into three columns, of which he himself commanded the centre, Colonel Trant the right, while the left, directed against Loison, was under General Ferguson. The centre marched against Laborde, who was posted on the elevated plain. This general, perceiving, at a glance, that his position was an unfavourable one, evaded the danger by falling rapidly back to the heights of Zambugeria, where he could only be approached by narrow paths, leading through deep ravines. A swarm of skirmishers, starting forward, soon plunged into the passes; and, spreading to the right and left, won their way among the rocks and tangled evergreens that overspread the steep ascent, and impeded their progress.

With still greater difficulty the supporting column followed, their formation being disordered in the confined and ragged passes, while the hollows echoed with the continual roar of musketry, and the shouts of the advancing troops were loudly answered by the enemy, while the curling smoke, breaking out from the side of the mountain, marked the progress of the assailants, and showed how stoutly the defence was maintained. The right of the 29th arrived first at the top; and, ere it could form, Col. Lake was killed, and a French company, falling on their flanks, broke through, carrying with them fifty or sixty prisoners. Thus pressed, this regiment fell back, and, re-forming under the hill, again advanced to the charge.

At the same time, General Ferguson poured his troops upon the other side of the devoted army. Laborde, seeing it impossible to effect a junction with Loison, or to maintain his present position, fell back,—commencing his retreat by alternate masses, and protecting his movements by vigorous charges of cavalry,—and halted at the Quinta de Bugagleira, where his scattered detachments rejoined him. From this place he marched all night, to gain the position of Montechique, leaving three guns on the field of battle, and the road to Torres Vedras open to the victors. The French lost six hundred men, killed and wounded, among the latter of which was the gallant Laborde himself.

Although the English were victors in this strife, the heroic defence of the French served to show them that they had no mean enemy to contend with. The personal enmity to Napoleon, and the violent party prejudices in England, were so great, that the most absurd stories as to the want of order and valour in his troops gained immediate credence there; and many of the English army believed that they had but to show themselves, and the French would fly. The bravery with which their attack was met was, of course, a matter of great surprise, and served as an efficient check to that rashness which this erroneous belief had engendered.

Instead of pursuing this victory, as Wellesley would have done, he was obliged to go to the seashore, to protect the landing of General Anstruthers and his troops. After having effected a junction with this general, he marched to Vimiero, where the French, under Junot, arrived on the 21st of August. The following brief and vivid sketch of this combat is taken from Alexander's Life of Wellington:

> Vimiero is a village, pleasantly situated in a gentle and quiet valley, through which flows the small river of Maceria. Beyond, and to the westward and northward of this village, rises a mountain, of which the western point reaches the sea; the eastern is separated by a deep ravine from the height, over which passes the road that leads from Lourinha and the northward to Vimiero. On this mountain were posted the chief part of the infantry, with eight pieces of artillery. General Hill's brigade was on the right, and Ferguson's on the left, having | one battalion on the heights, separated from them by the mountain. Towards the east and south of the town lay a mill, wholly commanded by the mountain on the west side, and commanding, also, the surrounding ground to the south and east, on which | General Fane was posted, with his riflemen, and the 50th regiment, and General Anstruthers' brigade, with the artillery, which had been ordered to that position during the night.

> About eight o'clock a picket of the enemy's horse was first seen on the heights, toward Lourinha; and, after pushing forward his scouts, soon appeared in full force, with the evident object of attacking the British. Immediately four brigades, from the mountains on

the east, moved across the ravine to the heights on the road to Lourinha, with three pieces of cannon. They were formed with their right resting upon these heights, and their left upon a ravine which separates the heights from a range at Maceria. On these heights were the Portuguese troops, and they were supported by General Crawford's brigade.

The enemy opened his attack, in strong columns, against the entire body of troops on this height. On the left they advanced, through the fire of the riflemen, close up to the 50th regiment, until they were checked and driven back by that regiment, at the point of the bayonet. The French infantry, in these divisions, was commanded by Laborde, Loison, and Kellerman, and the horse by General Margaron. Their attack was simultaneous, and like that of a man determined to conquer or to perish. Besides the conflict on the heights, the battle raged with equal fury on every part of the field. The possession of the road leading into Vimiero was disputed with persevering resolution, and especially where a strong body had been posted in the church-yard, to prevent the enemy forcing an entrance into the town. Up to this period of the battle the British had received and repulsed the attacks of the enemy, acting altogether on the defensive. But now they were attacked in flank by General Ackland's brigade, as it advanced to its position on the height to the left, while a brisk cannonade was kept up by the artillery on those heights.

The brunt of the attack was continued on the brigade of General Fane, but was bravely repulsed at all points. Once, as the French retired in confusion, a regiment of light dragoons pursued them with so little precaution, that they were suddenly set upon by the heavy cavalry of Margaron, and cut to pieces, with their gallant colonel at their head.

No less desperate was the encounter between Kellerman's column of reserve and the gallant 43rd, in their conflict for the vineyard adjoining the church. The advanced companies were at first driven back, with great slaughter; but, again rallying upon the next ranks, they threw themselves upon the head of a French column in a ravine, and, charging with the bayonet, put them to the rout. At length the vigour of the enemy's attack ceased. They, pressed on all sides by the British, had lost thirteen cannons and a great number of prisoners; but were still enabled to retire without confusion, owing to the protection of their numerous cavalry. An incident occurred in this battle, so highly characteristic of Highland courage, that I cannot refrain from quoting it. It is very common for the wounded to cheer their more fortunate comrades, as they pass on to the attack. A man named Stewart, the piper of the 71st regiment, was wounded in the thigh, very severely, at an early period of the action, and refused to be removed. He sat upon a bank, playing martial airs, during the remainder of the battle. As a party of his comrades were passing, he addressed them thus: 'Weel, my brave lads, I can gang na langer wi' ye a fightin', but ye shall na want music' On his return home, the Highland Society voted him a handsome set of pipes, with a flattering inscription engraved on them.

The total loss of the French was estimated at three thousand. Soon after the battle, General Kellerman presented himself, with a strong body of cavalry, at the outposts, and demanded an interview with the English general. The result of this interview was the famous convention of Cintra. By it, it was stipulated that Portugal should be delivered up to the British army, and the French should evacuate it, with arms and baggage, but not as prisoners of war; that the French should be transported, by the

British, into their own country; that the army should carry with it all its artillery, cavalry, arms, and ammunition, and the soldiers all their private property. It also provided that the Portuguese who had favoured the French party should not be punished.

According to the terms of this convention, Junot, on the 2nd of September, yielded the government of the capital. This suspension of military rule was followed by a wild scene of anarchy and confusion. The police disbanded of their own accord, and crime stalked abroad on every side. Lisbon was illuminated with thousands of little lamps, at their departure; and such was the state of the public mind, that Sir John Hope was obliged to make many and severe examples, before he succeeded in restoring order.

On the 13th, the Duke of Abrantes embarked, with his staff; and by the 30th of September only the garrisons of Elvas and Almeida remained in Portugal. This convention was very unpopular in England. The whole voice of the press was against it; and such was the state of feeling, that Sir Harry Burrard and Sir Hugh Dalrymple were both recalled, to present themselves before a court of inquiry, instituted for the occasion. After a minute investigation, these generals were declared innocent, but it was judged best to detain them at home.

Having seen Portugal under the control of the English, let us return to the affairs of Spain. Immediately after the battle of Baylen, which induced the retreat of Joseph from Madrid, Ferdinand was again declared king, and the pomp and rejoicings attendant on this event put an end to all business, except that of intrigue. The French were everywhere looked upon by the Spanish as a conquered foe, and they spent their time in the pageant of military triumphs and rejoicings, as though the enemy had already fled.

From this dream of fancied security Palafox was at length awakened by the appearance of a French corps, which retook Tudela, and pushed on almost to Saragossa. He appealed to the governing junta for aid and assistance. Much time was lost in intrigue and disputes, but at length the army was organized by appointing La Pena and Llamas to the charge. To supply the place usually occupied by the commander-in-chief, a board of general officers was projected, of which Castanos should be chief; but when some difficulty arose as to who the other members should be, this plan was deferred, with the remark, that "when the enemy was driven across the frontier, Castanos would have leisure to take his seat."

Of the state of the Spanish forces at this time, Napier says:

The idea of a defeat, the possibility of a failure, had never entered their minds. The government, evincing neither apprehension, nor activity, nor foresight, were contented if the people believed the daily falsehoods propagated relative to the enemy; and the people were content to be so deceived. The armies were neglected, even to nakedness; the soldier's constancy under privations cruelly abused; disunion, cupidity, incapacity, prevailed in the higher orders; patriotic ardour was visibly abating among the lower classes; the rulers were grasping, improvident, and boasting; the enemy powerful, the people insubordinate. Such were the allies whom the British found on their arrival in Spain.

Sir Arthur Wellesley had returned to Ireland, and the chief command was now given to Sir John Moore. This general, with the greatest celerity, marched his troops to the Spanish frontier, by the way of Almieda, having overcome almost insurmountable obstacles, arising from the state of affairs in Spain. Sir David Baird, with a force of ten thousand men, landed at Corunna, and also advanced to the contest; but they soon found that they were to meet an enemy with whom they were little able to cope.

Napoleon, with that energy so often displayed by him, when the greatness of the occasion required its exercise, collected, in an incredibly short space of time, an immense army of two hundred thousand men, most of them veterans who had partaken of the glories of Jena, Austerlitz, and Friedland. These were divided by the emperor into eight parts, called *corps d'armee*. At the head of each of them was placed one of his old and tried generals,—veterans on whom he could rely. The very names of Victor, Bessieres, Moncey, Lefebre, Mortier, Ney, St. Cyr, and Junot, speak volumes for the character of the army.

These troops were excited to the highest pitch of enthusiasm, by the emperor's address, as he passed through Paris, promising that he would head them in person, to drive the hideous leopard into the sea. What were the scattered and divided troops of the Spaniards, to contend with such a force? The grand French army reached Vittoria almost without an interruption. Blake was in position at Villarcayo, the Asturians were close at hand, Romana at Bilboa, and the Estremadurans at Burgos. With more valour than discretion, Blake made an attack upon Tornosa.

The enemy pretended to retreat. Blake, flushed with his apparent success, pursued them with avidity, when he suddenly came before twenty-five thousand men, under the Duke of Dantzic, and was furiously assailed. Blake, after a gallant defence, was obliged to retreat, in great confusion, upon Bilboa. He rallied, however, and was again in the field in a few days, fought a brave action with Villate, and was this time successful. With the vain-glory of his nation, he next attacked the strong city of Bilboa. Here, Marshal Victor gained a signal success, Blake losing two of his generals, and many of his men. Romana, who had joined Blake, renewed the action, with his veterans. They were made prisoners, but their brave chief escaped to the mountains.

Napoleon himself now left Bayonne, and directed his course into Spain. Only one day sufficed for his "arrival into Vittoria. At the gates of the city, a large procession, headed by the civil and military chiefs, met him, and wished to escort him to a splendid house prepared for his reception; but they were destined to a disappointment. Napoleon was there, not for pomp or show, but to direct, with his genius, the march of that army which he had raised. Jumping from his horse, he entered the first small inn he observed, and calling for his maps, and a report of the situation of the armies on both sides, proceeded to arrange the plan of his campaign. By daylight the next morning, his forces were in motion. The hastily levied troops of the Conde de Belvidere, himself a youth of only twenty years, were opposed to him. These were routed, with great slaughter,—one whole battalion, composed of the students of Salamanca and Lecon, fell to a man.

The army of the centre, under the command of Castanos, which was composed of fifty thousand men, with forty pieces of cannon, was totally routed at Tudela, by the French, under Lasnes and Ney; and now but one stronghold remained to the Spaniards, between the enemy and Madrid. This was the pass of the Somosierra. Here the Spanish army, under St. Juan, had posted their force. Sixteen pieces of artillery, planted in the neck of the pass, swept the road along the whole ascent, which was exceedingly steep and favourable for the defence.

The Spanish troops were disposed in lines, one above another; and when the French came on to the contest, they warmly returned their fire, and stood their ground. As yet, the grand battery had not opened its fire. This was waiting for the approach of the centre, under Napoleon himself. And now Napoleon, seeing that his troops were not advancing, rode slowly into the foot of the pass. The lofty mountain towered above him. Around its top hung a heavy fog, mingled with the curling smoke that was ascending from the mouth of all those cannon, rendering every object indistinct in the distance. Silently he gazed up the mountain.

A sudden thought strikes him. His practised eye has discerned, in a moment, what course to pursue. Turning to his brave Polish lancers, he orders them to charge up the causeway, and take the battery. They dashed onward. As they did so, the guns were turned full upon them, and their front ranks were levelled to the earth; but, ere they could reload, the Poles, nothing daunted, sprang over their dying comrades, and before the thick smoke, which enveloped them as a cloud, had dispersed, they rushed, sword in hand, upon the soldiers, and, cutting down the gunners, possessed themselves of the whole Spanish battery.

The panic became general. The Spaniards fled, leaving arms, ammunition, and baggage, to the enemy, and the road open to Madrid. Meanwhile, this city was in a state of anarchy seldom equalled. A multitude of peasants had entered the place. The pavements were taken up, the streets barricaded, and the houses pierced. They demanded arms and ammunition. These were supplied them. Then they pretended that sand had been mixed with the powder furnished. The Marquis of Perales, an old and worthy gentleman, was accused of the deed. The mob rushed to his house. They had no regard for age. They seized him by his silvery hair, and, dragging him down the steps, drew him through the streets until life was extinct.

For eight days the mob held possession of the city. No

man was safe; none dared assume authority, or even offer advice. Murder, and lust, and rapine, and cruelty, stalked fearlessly through the streets.

On the morning of the ninth, far away on the hills to the north-west, appeared a large body of cavalry, like a dark cloud overhanging the troubled city. At noon, the resistless emperor sat down before the gates of Madrid, and summoned the city to surrender. Calmness and quiet reigned in the French camp, but Madrid was struggling like a wild beast in the toils. Napoleon had no wish to destroy the capital of his brother's kingdom, but he was not to be trifled with. At midnight, a second summons was sent. It was answered by an equivocal reply, and responded to by the roar of cannon and the onset of the soldiery. This was an appeal not to be resisted. Madrid was in no state to stand a siege.

At noon, two officers, in Spanish uniform, and bearing a flag of truce, were observed approaching the French headquarters. They came to demand a suspension of arms, necessary, they said, to persuade the people to surrender. It was granted, and they returned to the city, with Napoleon's message. Before six o'clock in the morning, Madrid must surrender, or perish. Dissensions arose, but the voice of prudence prevailed, and the capital yielded. Napoleon was wise; he had no wish to goad a people already incensed to fury. The strictest discipline was maintained, and a soldier of his own guard was shot for having stolen a watch. Shops were re-opened, public amusements recommenced, and all was quiet. In six short weeks every Spanish army was dissipated. From St. Sebastian to the Asturias, from the Asturias to Talavera, from Talavera to the gates of Saragossa, all was submission, and beyond that boundary all was apathy or dread.

An assemblage of the nobles, the clergy, the corporations, and the tribunals, of Madrid, now waited on Napoleon at his headquarters, and presented an address, in which they expressed their desire to have Joseph return among them. Napoleon's reply was an exposition of what he had done and intended doing for Spain. Could the people but have yielded their prejudices, and submitted to his wise plans, what seas of tears and blood, what degradation and confusion, might have been spared to poor, unhappy Spain!

"I accept," said he, "the sentiments of the town of Madrid. I regret the misfortunes that have befallen it, and I hold it as a particular good fortune, that I am enabled to spare that city, and save it yet greater misfortunes. I have hastened to take measures to tranquillize all classes of citizens, knowing well that to all people and men uncertainty is intolerable.

''I have preserved the religious orders, but I have restrained the number of monks; no sane person can doubt that they are too numerous. Those who are truly called to this vocation, by the grace of God, will remain in the convents; those who have lightly, or for worldly motives, adopted it, will have their existence secured among the secular ecclesiastics, from the surplus of the convents.

"I have provided for the wants of the most interesting and useful of the clergy, the parish priests.

"I have abolished that tribunal against which Europe and the age alike exclaimed. Priests ought to guide consciences, but they should not exercise any exterior or corporal jurisdiction over men.

"I have taken the satisfaction which was due to myself and to my nation, and the part of vengeance is completed. Ten of the principal criminals bend their heads before her; but for all others there is absolute and entire pardon.

"I have suppressed the rights usurped by the nobles

during civil wars, when the kings have been too often obliged to abandon their own rights, to purchase tranquillity and the repose of the people.

"I have suppressed the feudal rights, and every person can now establish inns, mills, ovens, weirs, and fisheries, and give good play to their industry, only observing the laws and customs of the place. The self-love, the riches, and the prosperity, of a small number of men, were more hurtful to your agriculture than the heats of the dog-days.

"As there is but one God, there should be in one estate but one justice; wherefore all the particular jurisdictions have been usurped, and, being contrary to the national rights, I have destroyed them. I have also made known to all persons that which each can have to fear, and that which they may hope for.

"The English armies I will drive from the Peninsula. Saragossa, Valencia, Seville, shall be reduced, either by persuasion or by force of arms.

"There is no obstacle capable of retarding, for any length of time, my will; but that which is above my power is to constitute the Spaniards a nation, under the orders of a king, if they continue to be imbued with divisions, and hatred towards France, such as the English partisans and the enemies of the continent have instilled into them. I cannot establish a nation, a king, and Spanish independence, if that king is not sure of the affection and fidelity of his subjects.

"The Bourbons can never reign again in Europe. The divisions in the royal family were concerted by the English. It "was not either King Charles or his favourite, but the Duke of Infantado, the instrument of England, that was upon the point of overturning the throne. The papers recently found in his house prove this. It was the preponderance of England that they wished to establish in Spain. Insensate project! which would have produced a long war without end, and caused torrents of blood to be shed.

"No power influenced by England can exist upon this continent. If any desire it, their desire is folly, and sooner or later will ruin them. I shall be obliged to govern Spain; and it will be easy for me to do it, by establishing a viceroy in each province. However, I will not refuse to concede my rights of conquest to the king, and to establish him in Madrid, when the thirty thousand citizens assemble in the churches, and on the holy sacrament take an oath, not with the mouth alone, but with the heart, and without any Jesuitical restriction, to be true to the king,—to love and support him. Let the priests from the pulpit and in the confessional, the tradesmen in their correspondence and in their discourses, inculcate these sentiments in the people; then I will relinquish my rights of conquest, and I will place the king upon the throne, and I will take a pleasure in showing myself the faithful friend of the Spaniards.

"The present generation may differ in opinions. Too many passions have been excited; but your descendants will bless me, as the regenerator of the nation. They will mark my sojourn among you as memorable days, and from those days they will date the prosperity of Spain. These are my sentiments. Go, consult your fellow-citizens; choose your part, but do it frankly, and exhibit only true colours."

The ten criminals were the Dukes of Infantado, of Hijah, of Mediniceli, and Ossuna; Marquis Santa Cruz, Counts Fernan, Minez, and Altamira; Prince of Castello Franco,

Pedro Cevallos, and the Bishop of St. Ander, were proscribed, body and goods, as traitors to France and Spain.

Napoleon now made dispositions indicating a vast plan of operations. But, vast as his plan of campaign appears, it was not beyond the emperor's means; for, without taking into consideration his own genius, activity and vigour, there were upon his muster-rolls above three hundred and thirty thousand men and above sixty thousand horse; two hundred pieces of field artillery followed his corps to battle; and as many more remained in reserve.

Of this great army, however, only two hundred and fifty thousand men and fifty thousand horses were actually under arms with the different regiments, while above thirty thousand were detached or in garrisons, preserving tranquillity in the rear, and guarding the communications of the active forces. The remainder were in hospitals. Of the whole host, two hundred and thirteen thousand were native Frenchmen, the residue were Poles, Germans and Italians; thirty-five thousand men and five thousand horses were available for fresh enterprise, without taking a single man from the lines of communication.

The fate of the Peninsula hung, at this moment, evidently upon a thread; and the deliverance of that country was due to other causes than the courage, the patriotism, or the constancy, of the Spaniards. The strength and spirit of Spain was broken; the enthusiasm was null, except in a few places, in consequence of the civil wars, and intestinal divisions incited by the monks and British hirelings; and the emperor was, with respect to the Spaniards, perfectly master of operations. He was in the centre of the country; he held the capital, the fortresses, the command of the great lines of communication between the provinces; and on the wide military horizon no cloud interrupted his view, save the city of Saragossa on the one side, and the British army on the other.

"Sooner or later," said the emperor, and with truth, "Saragossa must fall."

The subjugation of Spain seemed inevitable, when, at this instant, the Austrian war broke out, and this master-spirit was suddenly withdrawn. England then put forth all her vast resources, and the genius and vigour of Sir John Moore, aided, most fortunately, by the absence of Napoleon, and the withdrawal of the strength of his army for the subjugation of the Peninsula; and it was delivered from the French, after oceans of blood had been spilt and millions of treasure wasted, to fall into the hands of the not less tyrannical and oppressive English. "But through what changes of fortune, by what unexpected helps, by what unlooked-for events,—under what difficulties, by whose perseverance, and in despite of whose errors,—let posterity judge; for in that judgment," says Napier, "only will impartiality and justice be found."

Tidings having reached the emperor that the Austrian army was about to invade France, he recalled a large portion of his army, and appointing his brother Joseph to be his lieutenant-general, he allotted separate provinces to each *corps d'armee*, and directing the imperial guard to hasten to France, he returned to Valladolid, where he received the addresses of the nobles and deputies of Madrid, and. other great towns; and after three days' delay, he departed himself, with scarcely any escort, but with such astonishing speed as to frustrate the designs which some Spaniards had, in some way, formed against his person.

The general command of the French army in Spain was left with Soult, assisted by Ney. This gallant general, bearing the title, of the Duke of Dalmatia, commenced his pursuit of the English army with a vigour that marked his eager desire to finish the campaign in a manner suitable to its brilliant opening. Sir John Moore had arrived in Salamanca by the middle of November, and on the 23rd the other divisions of

the army had arrived at the stations assigned them. Sir David
Baird had already reported himself at Astorga, when Moore
received positive information that the French had entered
Valladolid in great force. And this place was only three days'
march distant from the British. At a glance, the great mind of
Moore comprehended the full difficulty of his critical situation. In the heart of a foreign country, unsupported by the
Spanish government, his army wanting the very necessaries
of life, he found himself obliged to commence that retreat in
winter, over mountains covered with snow, which proved so
fatal to the British army, or wait to meet the French troops,
flushed with victory, and sustained by an overwhelming
force. In vain he appealed to the junta of Salamanca for
aid. In vain he endeavoured to arouse the spirit of patriotism, which had shone forth so brightly in the first days of
the insurrection. Instead of aiding him either to advance
or retreat, they endeavoured to direct him what course to
pursue; and painted, with true Spanish pride and hyper-
bole, in glowing colours, what their armies had done, and
what they could do. His camp was therefore struck, and he
retreated through the rocks of Gallicia, closely followed by
the pursuing army.

   Whenever the advance guards of the enemy approached,
the British rallied with vigour, and sustained their reputation for bravery; but they displayed a lamentable want of
discipline in all other parts of their conduct. The weather
was tempestuous; the roads miserable; the commissariat was
utterly defective, and the very idea that they were retreating
was sufficient to crush the spirits of the soldiery.

   At Bembibre, although the English well knew that the
French were close behind, they broke into the immense
wine-vaults of that city. All effort by their officers to control them was utterly useless. Hundreds became so inebri-
ated as to be unable to proceed, and Sir John Moore was

obliged to proceed without them. Scarcely had the reserve marched out of the village, when the French cavalry appeared. In a moment the road was filled with the miserable stragglers, who came crowding after the troops, some with shrieks of distress and wild gestures, others with brutal exclamations; while many, overcome with fear, threw away their arms, and those who preserved them were too stupidly intoxicated to fire, and kept reeling to and fro, alike insensible to their danger and disgrace. The enemy's horsemen, perceiving this, bore at a gallop through the disorderly mob, cutting to the right and left as they passed, and riding so close to the columns that the infantry were forced to halt in order to protect them.

At Villa Franca even greater excesses were committed; the magazines were plundered, the bakers driven. away from the ovens, the wine-stores forced, the doors of the houses were broken, and the scandalous insubordination of the soldiers was, indeed, a disgrace to the army. Moore endeavoured to arrest this disorder, and caused one man, taken in the act of plundering a magazine, to be hanged. He also endeavoured to send despatches to Sir David Baird, directing him to Corunna, instead of Vigo; but his messenger became drunk and lost his despatches, and this act cost the lives of more than four hundred men, besides a vast amount of suffering to the rest of the army. An unusual number of women and children had been allowed to accompany the army, and their sufferings were, indeed, dreadful to witness. Clark, in his history of the war, gives a heart-rending account of the horrors of this retreat.

The mountains were now covered with snow; there was neither provision to sustain nature nor shelter from the rain and snow, nor fuel for fire to keep the vital heat from total extinction, nor place where the weary and footsore could rest for a single hour in safety. The soldiers, barefooted, harassed and weakened by their excesses, were dropping to the rear by hundreds; while broken carts, dead animals, and the piteous appearance of women, with children, straggling or falling exhausted in the snow, completed the dreadful picture. It was still attempted to carry forward some of the sick and wounded;—the beasts that drew them failed at every step, and they were left to perish amid the snows."

"I looked around," says an officer, "when we had hardly gained the highest point of those slippery precipices, and saw the rear of the army winding along the narrow road. I saw their way marked by the wretched people, who lay on all sides, expiring from fatigue and the severity of the cold, their bodies reddening in spots the white surface of the ground."

A Portuguese bullock-driver, who had served the English from the first day of their arrival, was seen on his knees amid the snow, dying, in the attitude and act of prayer. He had, at least, the consolations of religion, in his dying hour. But the English soldiers gave utterance to far different feelings, in their last moments. Shame and anger mingled with their groans and imprecations on the Spaniards, who had, as they said, betrayed them. Mothers found their babes sometimes frozen in their arms, and helpless infants were seen seeking for nourishment from the empty breasts of their dead a mothers.

One woman was taken in labour upon the mountain. She lay down at the turning of an angle, rather more sheltered than the rest of the way from the icy sleet which drifted along; there she was found dead, and two babes which she had brought forth struggling in the snow. A blanket was thrown over her, to hide her from sight,—the only burial that could be afforded; and the infants were given in charge to a woman who came up in one of the carts, little likely, as it was, that they could survive such a journey.

Soult hung close on the rear of this unfortunate army, and pursued them until they reached Corunna, on the 12th of January. As the morning dawned, the weary and unfortunate general, saddened by the dark scenes through which he had passed, sensible that the soldiers were murmuring at their retreat, unsupported by his Spanish allies, and well aware that rumour and envy and misunderstanding would be busy with his name in his own native land, appeared on the heights that overhung the town. With eager and anxious gaze, he turned to the harbour, hoping to perceive there his fleet, which he had ordered to sail from Vigo. But the same moody fortune which had followed him during his whole career pursued him here. The wintry sun looked down upon the foaming ocean, and only the vast expanse of water met his view. The fleet, detained by contrary winds, was nowhere visible; and once more he was obliged to halt with his forces, and take up quarters.

The army was posted on a low ridge, and waited for the French to come up. The sadness of the scene was by no means passed. Here, stored in Corunna, was a large quantity of ammunition, sent over from England, and for the want of which both the Spanish and English forces had suffered, and which Spanish idleness and improvidence had suffered to remain here for months, unappropriated. This must now be destroyed, or fall into the possession of the enemy. Three miles from the town were piled four thousand barrels of powder on a hill, and a smaller quantity at some distance from it.

On the morning of the 13th, the inferior magazine blew up, with a terrible noise, and shook the houses in the town;

but when the train reached the great store, there ensued a crash like the bursting forth of a volcano;—the earth trembled for miles, the rocks were torn from their bases, and the agitated waters rolled the vessels, as in a storm; a vast column of smoke and dust, shooting out fiery sparks from its sides, arose perpendicularly and slowly to a great height, and then a shower of stones and fragments of all kinds, bursting out of it with a roaring sound, killed many persons who remained too near the spot. Stillness, slightly interrupted by the lashing of the waves on the shore, succeeded, and then the business of the day went on. The next scene was a sad one. All the horses of the army were collected together, and, as it was impossible to embark them in face of the enemy, they were ordered to be shot. These poor animals would otherwise have been distributed among the French cavalry, or used as draft-horses.

On the 14th, the transports from Vigo arrived. The dismounted cavalry, the sick and wounded, the best horses, belonging to the officers, which had been saved, and fifty-two pieces of artillery, were embarked during the night, only retaining twelve guns on shore, ready for action. And now the closing scene of this sad drama was rapidly approaching, giving a melancholy but graceful termination to the campaign.

On the night of the 15th, everything was shipped that was destined to be removed, excepting the fighting men. These were intending to embark, as soon as the darkness should permit them to move without being perceived, on the night of the 16th; but in the afternoon the French troops drew up, and offered battle. This the English general would not refuse, and the action soon became general.

The battle was advancing, with varied fortune, when Sir John Moore, who was earnestly watching the result of the battle in the village of Elvina, received his death-wound. A spent cannon-ball struck him on his breast. The shock threw him from his horse, with violence; but he rose again, in a sitting posture, his countenance unchanged, and his steadfast eye still fixed on the regiments before him, and betraying no signs of pain. In a few moments, when satisfied that his troops were gaining ground, his countenance brightened, and he suffered himself to be carried to the rear. Then was seen the dreadful nature of his hurt. The shoulder was shattered to pieces; the arm was hanging by a piece of skin; the ribs over the heart were broken and bared of flesh, and the muscles of the breast torn into long strips, which were interlaced by their recoil from the dragging shot.

As the soldiers placed him in a blanket, his sword got entangled, and the hilt entered the wound. Captain Hardinge, a staff officer, who was near, attempted to take it off; but the dying man stopped him, saying, "It is as well as it is; I had rather it should go out of the field with me." And in that manner, so becoming to a soldier, he was borne from the fight by his devoted men, who went up the hill weeping as they went. The blood flowed fast, and the torture of his wound was great; yet, such was the unshaken firmness of his mind, that those about him judged, from the resolution of his countenance, that his hurt was not mortal, and said so to him. He looked steadfastly at the wound for a few moments, and then said, "No,—I feel that to be impossible."

Several times he caused his attendants to turn around, that he might behold the field of battle; and, when the firing indicated the advance of the British, he discovered his satisfaction, and permitted his bearers to proceed. Being brought to his lodgings, the surgeon examined his wound, but there was no hope. The pain increased, and he spoke with great difficulty. Addressing an old friend, he said, "You know that I always wished to die this way."

Again he asked if the enemy were defeated; and being

told that they were, observed, "It is a great satisfaction to me that we have beaten the French." Once, when he spoke of his mother, he became agitated. It was the only time. He inquired after his friends and officers who had survived the battle, and did not even now forget to recommend those whose merit entitled them to promotion. His strength I failed fast; and life was almost extinct, when he exclaimed, as if in that dying hour the veil of the future had been lifted, and he had seen the baseness of his posthumous calumniators, "I hope the people of England will be satisfied; I hope my country will do me justice." In a few minutes afterwards he died, and his corpse, wrapped in a military cloak, was interred by the officers of his staff, in the citadel of Corunna. The guns of the enemy paid his funeral honours, and the valiant Duke of Dalmatia, with a characteristic nobleness, raised a monument to his memory. The following is so beautiful and touching a description of his burial, that we cannot refrain from quoting it, even though it may be familiar to most of our readers. It was written by the Rev, Charles Wolfe, of Dublin.

Not a drum was heard—not a funeral note—
As his corpse to the ramparts we hurried;
Not a soldier discharged his farewell shot
O'er the grave where our hero was buried.

We buried him darkly, at dead of night,
The sods with our bayonets turning,
By the struggling moonbeams' misty light,
And the lantern dimly burning.

No useless coffin enclosed his breast,
Nor in sheet nor in shroud we wound him;
But he lay like a warrior taking his rest,
With his martial cloak around him.

Few and short were the prayers we said,
And we spoke not a word of sorrow;
But we steadfastly gazed on the face of the dead,
And bitterly thought of the morrow.

We thought, as we hollowed his narrow bed,
And smoothed down his lonely pillow,
That the foe and the stranger would tread o'er his head,
And we far away on the billow.

Lightly they'll talk of the spirit that's gone,
And o'er his cold ashes upbraid him;
But little he'll reek, if they let him sleep on
In the grave where a Briton has laid him.

But half of our heavy task was done,
When the clock struck the hour for retiring
And we heard the distant and random gun
Of the enemy, suddenly firing.

Slowly and sadly we laid him down,
From the field of his fame, fresh and gory;
We carved not a line—we raised not a stone—
But we left him alone with his glory.

The battle was continued until dark, under great disadvantages on the part of the French, owing to the difficulty they experienced in dragging their heavy cannon on to the heights, and their small amount of ammunition. The French loss has been estimated at three thousand, and the British at eight hundred; but the loss of the French was undoubtedly exaggerated.

The English availed themselves of the darkness and the confusion among the enemy to embark their troops; and so complete were the arrangements of Sir John Hope, who succeeded to the command, that it was all effected, without delay or difficulty, before morning. The wounded were provided for, and the fleet, although fired upon by the French, sailed on the 17th for their home in England.

But their trials were not yet closed. It was Sir John Moore's intention to have proceeded to Vigo, that he might restore order before he sailed for England; but the fleet went directly home from Corunna, and a terrible storm scattered it, many ships were wrecked, and the remainder, driving up the channel, were glad to put into any port. The soldiers thus thrown on shore were spread all over the country. Their haggard appearance, ragged clothing, and dirty accoutrements, struck a people only used to the daintiness of parade with surprise. A deadly fever, the result of anxiety and of the sudden change from fatigue to the confinement of a ship, filled the hospitals at every port with officers and soldiers, and the terrible state of the army was the all-absorbing topic of conversation.

CHAPTER 3

The War Rages On

Having closed the history of this unfortunate army, let us now return to Spain. Joseph had returned, a nominal king, to Madrid. More than twenty-six thousand heads of families had come forward, of their own accord, and sworn, by the host, that they desired his presence amongst them. The marshals, under his directions, were pursuing the conquest of Spain with vigour. Though Joseph was nominally lieutenant-general, Soult was in reality at the head of operations. A modern writer, speaking of these two commanders, says Soult was crippled in all his movements, his sound policy neglected, and his best combinations thwarted, by Joseph. His operations in Andalusia and Estramadura, and the firmness with which he resisted the avarice of Joseph, all exhibited his well-balanced character. In Andalusia he firmly held his ground, although hedged in with hostile armies, and surrounded by an insurgent population, while a wide territory had to be covered with his troops.

King Joseph could not comprehend the operations of such a mind as Soult's, and constantly impeded his success. When, without ruin to his army, the stubborn marshal could yield to his commands, he did; but where the king's projects would plunge him into irredeemable errors, he openly and firmly withstood them. The anger and threats of Joseph were alike in vain. The inflexible old soldier professed his willingness to obey, but declared he would not, with his eyes open, commit a great military blunder. King Joseph would despatch loud and vehement complaints to Napoleon, but the emperor knew too well the ability of Soult to heed them. Had the latter been on the Spanish throne, the country would long before have been subdued, and the French power established.

We shall not enter into detail of all the operations in Spain. A short account of some of the principal battles we will give; and, as we have already detailed the first siege of Saragossa, our readers may perhaps like to know the final fate of this devoted city. We quote from Headley's description of the second siege.

> The siege at Saragossa had been successively under the command of Moncey and Junot. The camp was filled with murmurs and complaints. For nearly a month they had environed the town in vain. Assault after assault had been made; and from the 2nd of January, when Junot took the command, till the arrival of Lannes in the latter part of the month, every night had been distinguished by bloody fights; and yet the city remained unconquered. Lannes paid no heed to the murmurs and complaints around him, but immediately, by the promptitude and energy of his actions, infused courage into the hearts of the desponding soldiery.
>
> The decision he was always wont to carry into battle was soon visible in the siege. The soldiers poured to the assault with firmer purpose, and fought with more resolute courage. The apathy which had settled down on the army was dispelled. New life was given to every movement; and on the 27th, amid the tolling of the tower-bell, warning the people to the defence, a grand assault was made, and, after a most sanguinary conflict,

the walls of the town were carried, and the French soldiers fortified themselves in the convent at St. Joseph's. Unyielding to the last, the brave Saragossans fought on, and, amid the pealing of the tocsin, rushed up to the very mouths of the cannons, and perished by hundreds and by thousands in the streets of the city. Every house was a fortress, and around its walls were separate battlefields, where deeds of frantic valour were done.

Day after day did these single-handed fights continue, while famine and pestilence walked the city at noonday, and slew faster than the swords of the enemy. The dead lay piled up in every street, and on the thick heaps of the slain the living mounted, and fought with the energy of despair for their homes and their liberty. In the midst of this incessant firing by night and by day, and hand to hand fights on the bodies of the slain, ever and anon a mine would explode, blowing the living and dead, friend and foe, together in the air. An awful silence would succeed for a moment, and then, over the groans of the dying, would ring again the rallying cry of the; brave inhabitants. The streets ran torrents of blood, and the stench of putrefied bodies loaded the air.

Thus, for three weeks, did the fight and butchery go on, within the city walls, till the soldiers grew dispirited and ready to give up the hope of spoils, if they could escape the ruin that encompassed them. Yet theirs was a comfortable lot to that of the besieged. Shut up in the cellars with the dead, pinched with famine, while the pestilence rioted without mercy and without resistance, they heard around them the incessant bursting of bombs, and thunder of artillery, and explosions of mines, and crash of falling houses, till the city shook, night and day, as within the grasp of an earthquake. Thousands fell daily, and the town was a mass of ruins. Yet, unconquered and apparently unconquerable, the inhabitants struggled on.

Out of the dens they had made for themselves among the ruins, and from the cellars where there were more dead than living, men would crawl to fight, who looked more like spectres than warriors. Women would work the guns, and, musket in hand, advance fearlessly to the charge; and hundreds thus fell, fighting for their homes and their firesides. Amid this scene of devastation,—against this prolonged and almost hopeless struggle of weeks,—against the pestilence that had appeared in his own army, and was mowing down his own troops,—and, above all, against the increased murmurs and now open clamours of the soldiers, declaring that the siege must be abandoned till reinforcements could come up,—Lannes remained unshaken and untiring. The incessant roar and crash around him, the fetid air, the exhausting toil, the carnage and the pestilence, could not change his iron will. He had decreed that Saragossa—which had heretofore baffled every attempt to take it—should fall. At length, by a vigorous attempt, he took the convent of St. Laran, in the suburbs of the town, and planted his artillery there, which soon levelled the city around it with the ground.

To finish this work of destruction by one grand blow, he caused six mines to be run under the main street of the city, each of which was charged with three thousand pounds of powder. But before the time appointed for their explosion arrived, the town capitulated. The historians of this siege describe the appearance of the city and its inhabitants, after the surrender, as inconceivably horrible. With only a single wall between them and the enemy's trenches, they had endured a siege of nearly two months by forty thousand men, and continued to resist after famine and pestilence began to slay faster than the enemy. Thirty thousand cannon-balls and sixty thousand bombs had fallen in the city, and fifty-four thousand of the inhabitants had perished. Six thousand only had fallen in combat, while forty-eight thousand had been the prey of the pestilence. After the town had capitulated, but twelve thousand were found able to bear arms, and they looked more like spectres issuing from the tomb than like living warriors.

Saragossa was taken; but what a capture! As Lannes rode through the streets at the head of his victorious army, he looked only on a heap of ruins, while six thousand unburied corpses lay in his path. Sixteen thousand lay sick, while on the living famine had written more dreadful characters than death had traced on the fallen. Infants lay on the breasts of their dead mothers, striving in vain to draw life from bosoms that would never throb again.

Attenuated forms, with haggard faces and sunken eyes and cheeks, wandered around among the dead to search for their friends; corpses, bloated with famine, lay stretched across the threshold of their dwellings, and strong-limbed men went staggering over the pavements, weak from want of food, or struck with the pestilence. Woe was in every street, and the silence in the dwellings was more eloquent than the loudest cries and groans.

Death and famine and the pestilence had been there, in every variety of form and suffering. But the divine form of Liberty had been there too, walking amid those mountains of corpses and ruins of homes, shedding her light through the subterranean apartments of the wretched, and, with her cheering voice, animating the thrice-conquered, yet still unconquered, to another effort, and blessing the dying as they prayed for their beloved city. But she was at last compelled to take her departure, and the bravest city of modern Europe sunk in bondage. Still her example lives, and shall live to the end of time, nerving the patriot to strike and suffer for his home and freedom, and teaching man everywhere how to die in defending the right.

A wreath of glory surrounds the brow of Saragossa, fadeless as the memory of her brave defenders. Before their achievements,—the moral grandeur of their firm struggle, and the depth and intensity of their sufferings,—the bravery and perseverance of the French sink into forgetfulness. Yet theirs was no ordinary task, and it was by no ordinary means that it was executed.

The English had by no means relinquished their designs upon the Peninsula. The successes of Napoleon and his victorious army but served to stimulate their hatred of the French, and spur them on to further efforts. Another army was accordingly collected, and placed under the command of Sir Arthur Wellesley, who landed in Lisbon on the 22nd of April, 1809. The force under his command was fourteen thousand five hundred infantry, fifteen hundred cavalry, and twenty-four pieces of artillery. The passage of the river Duero was his first contest with the French. In this he was successful, and his success opened to him the gates of Oporto. Soon after occurred the celebrated battle of Talavera.

King Joseph was himself nominally at the head of his troops; but Marshal Victor was, in reality, the leader. Victor and Soult had both laid their plans before the king, and urged them with all the eloquence they were capable of. So sure was Victor of the victory, should his advice be followed, that he j said that, if his plans should fail, all military science was useless. The event proved, however, that Soult was correct.

The morning dawned beautifully clear, but a July sun poured down its burning heat, until the soldiers were glad to seek shelter from its rays in the quiet shade. Between the camps of the two armies flowed a little murmuring rivulet, and, as the French and English met there to slake their thirst, pleasant words passed between them. Familiar conversation, the light laugh and the gay jest, were heard on every side.

But, about one o'clock, the deep rolling of drums along the French lines announced to the allies that the hour had come when those who had met to slake their thirst in those quiet waters were soon to mingle to quell in blood their thirst for strife. They, too, prepared for combat; and, when the loud booming of the guns gave the signal that the battle was commenced, eighty cannon opened their destructive fire, and the light troops went sweeping onward with the rapidity of a thunder-cloud over the heavens, while the deep, dark columns marched sternly after, and charged, with terrible strength, the English lines.

Then all along their fronts the deep-mouthed guns opened their well-directed fire, and the infantry responded to the furious attack with their rapid volleys, as they closed around the head of the advancing columns, enveloping them in one sheet of flame, that streamed like billows along their sides. It was too much for human courage to endure; and, after bravely breasting the storm, they were obliged to fall back in disorder.

After various successes and reverses, the French seemed about to gain the day. The English centre was broken, and Victor's columns marching triumphantly through it. Just at this juncture, when the English were scattering on every side, Colonel Donellan, anxious to save the honour of his army, was seen advancing through the disordered masses, at the head of the 48th regiment. The retiring masses on every side pressed hard against these brave soldiers, and it seemed, at first, as though they must be carried away by them; but, wheeling back by companies, they opened to let the fugitives pass, and then, pursuing their proud and beautiful line, they marched straight upon the pursuing columns on the right side, and poured their rapid fire into the dense ranks.

Closing on the foe with steadiness and firmness, these few soldiers arrested the progress of the entire mass. Then their artillery opened its fire upon them, and the cavalry rallied, and rode round to charge their flanks; and, after a short and earnest warfare, the tide of success turned, and victory, which seemed a moment before in the hands of the French, was wrested from their grasp, amid the loud shouts and earnest cheerings of the British. Their troops retired in good order to their former position, and at six o'clock the battle had closed. And now, as both parties were preparing to remove their wounded, and pay the last sad duties to the dead, one of those terrible events occurred which sometimes come to shock the human soul, and overrun a cup of misery already full.

Hardly had the last troops withdrawn from the scene of contest, when the long dry grass took fire, and one broad flame swept furiously over the field, wrapping the dead and wounded together in its fiery mantle. The shrieks of the scorched and writhing victims, that struggled up through the thick folds of smoke that rolled darkly over them, were far more appalling than the uproar of battle, and carried consternation to every heart that heard. Two thousand men were killed on both sides, and eight thousand wounded.

Soon after, the army effected a junction with Soult, and

Sir Arthur Wellesley was obliged to retreat. He obtained, however, a promise from the Spanish general that the English wounded should be removed from the hospitals of Talavera to some other place. But this promise, like too many others, was shamefully violated; and he left the place, abandoning them all to the mercy of the enemy.

When Victor entered the town, he found the public square covered with the sick and maimed of both armies, scattered around on the pavement, without any one to care for them. He immediately sent his soldiers into the houses, commanding the inhabitants to receive the wounded sufferers. He ordered that one English and one French soldier should be lodged together,—thus softening the asperities of war, and setting an example to his foes which they would have done well to follow.

If the Spanish had refused to care for the sick and wounded of their allies, they showed scarcely more consideration for the men on whose success their own safety depended. They refused to supply them with provisions. The soldiers were weakened by hunger, and the sick dying for want of necessary succour. Half a pound of wheat in the grain, and, twice a week, a few ounces of flour, with a quarter of a pound of goat's flesh, formed the sole subsistence of men and officers. The goats were caught and killed by the troops; and it was so difficult to procure even these, that the mere offal of a goat would bring three or four dollars.

Sir Arthur's warm remonstrances to the Spanish junta were answered only by promises. The soldiers were murmuring at their bad treatment; and, when pestilence broke out in the army, and five thousand men died in their hospitals, Wellesley, deeming it useless to struggle longer against the force of circumstances, judged it best again to evacuate Spain, and withdraw his troops into Portugal. However lightly the English had, in anticipation, regarded the bravery of the French troops, experience—that stern and truthful monitor —had taught them that they were an enemy not to despised, and that Soult, their chief commander, was as skilful, and, as a tactician, fully equal to Wellington.

Many English writers, in speaking of Wellington, have drawn a parallel between him and Napoleon because he was commander-in-chief when the battle of Waterloo was won. Yet this long struggle between; the English general and Soult, in Spain, in which he was as often defeated as conqueror, shows conclusively that the French and English commanders were well matched,—that there was little to choose between them; and who would think, even for a moment, of instituting a comparison of equality between Napoleon and Soult?

We cannot follow the Spaniards, in all their operations, after the English forces had been withdrawn; marked, as they often were, by want of courage, and oftener by want of skill and foresight in their arrangements. The Partida warfare was now instituted, and many of the French troops were cut off in this way; yet the system was a decided injury to Spain. The heroic defence of Saragossa, already recorded, and the almost equally courageous one of Gerona, rise as bright spots on the dark page of Spanish history, and are well worthy of a name and place in this history. Most of the siege of Grerona we shall take the liberty to extract from Tucker's Life of Wellington.

> Gerona is a city of Catalonia, situate on the little river Onar. It is protected by four forts, upon the high ground above it. Its principal defence, however, was the citadel, called the Monjuie. This is a square fort, two hundred and forty yards in length on each side, with four bastions. The garrisons consisted of three thousand four hundred men, commanded by Mariano

Alvarez,—a man at once noble, brave, and humane. Alvarez, who knew that he could place small dependence on reinforcements from without, gave every encouragement to the feelings of the citizens to defend their town to the last extremity. For this purpose, he formed them into eight companies of one hundred men each.

Nor was the enthusiasm of the defence shared alone by the men. Maids and matrons also enrolled themselves in an association, which they termed the Company of St. Barbara, to perform whatever lay in their power. Alvarez knew full well the power which superstition would exert on the minds of the bigoted Spaniards. He, therefore, invested St. Narcis, the patron saint of the Geronans, with the insignia of generalissimo of all their forces, by land and by sea. This was done on the Sabbath; and the shrine of the saint was opened, and a general's staff, a sword and richly-ornamented belt, were deposited with his holy relics. Such was the joy and excitement of the Spaniards, that one of their writers says, "It seemed as if the glory of the Lord had descended and filled the church, manifesting that their devotion was approved and blessed by heaven."

A proclamation was also issued by Alvarez, forbidding all persons, of whatever rank, from speaking of capitulation, on pain of immediate death. This was received, both by the garrison and people, with acclamation.

The city was closely invested by eighteen thousand French, under the command of General Verdier, on the 6th of May, on the heights of Casa Roca, where they erected a battery of eleven mortars, and began to form their first line of circumvallation. The garrison was too weak to make a sally, or otherwise prevent them. A flag of truce was sent, with the conditions on which the French would leave the city; but the only reply it drew forth was, that the Geronans would hold no communication with the French, but at the cannon's mouth. At one o'clock on the morning of June 14th, the bombardment commenced. As soon as the first shell struck, the loud tones of the *generale* resounded through the streets, and every one flew to his post. The female Company of St. Barbara, so far from shrinking from danger, sought everywhere those spots where most was anticipated.

What bravery or daring could do was done; yet two castles were yielded up, after a brave but vain resistance. Palamas was also carried by assault. Very few of the garrison escaped, and those only by throwing themselves into the sea. In July, three batteries kept up an incessant fire upon three sides of the Monjuie. By one of these discharges the angle on which the Spanish flag was planted was cut off, and the flag prostrated into the ditch below. In an instant, a man was lowered down from the walls to regain it. Balls fell like hail around him; yet, apparently unmindful of the dangers to which he was exposed, he calmly descended, and, having recovered the prostrate banner, returned to his comrades unhurt, and again hoisted it on the walls.

A breach was now made in the walls so wide that forty men might enter abreast. The works progressed with more rapidity, as the fire of the besieged had entirely ceased. It was not that Gerona was conquered, but, finding that their ammunition was growing short, they prudently reserved it until the nearer approach of the enemy should make it more efficient. On the morning of the 8th, about three o'clock, the French, under cover of a most tremendous bombardment, again assaulted the city.

Six thousand men marched up to the breach, and

endeavoured to rush through; but, concealed there in the ruins of the ravelin, lay a mortar, which discharged five hundred musket-balls every shot. As they advanced, it was turned upon them, and their way was soon impeded by the slain. Three times during that day the assault was repeated, with the utmost resolution, by the assailants; and three times were they obliged to retire before the heroic defenders of Gerona, leaving sixteen hundred men lifeless on the field of battle. But the effect of that dreadful attack was severely felt by the besieged. The tower of St. Juan had been blown up, and only twenty-three of its brave little garrison remained alive.

An instance of extraordinary heroism, in a youthful drummer, which occurred during the assault, serves to be recorded. His name was Luciana Ancio, and he belonged to the artillery. He was stationed to give the alarm, when a shell was thrown. A ball struck his leg off to the knee, and felled him to the ground. Some women, who saw him fall, hastened to remove him to a place of greater safety; but he refused, saying, "No, no! My arms are left, and I can still beat the drum to give my comrades warning in time to save themselves." Heaven seemed to smile upon his bravery; for he alone, of all those who suffered an amputation of the thigh during the siege, recovered.

The Company of St. Barbara were everywhere to be seen, covered with dust and blood, under the burning heat of a July sun. Those courageous women, through an incessant fire of the batteries and the musketry, carried water and wine to the soldiers, and bore back the wounded. Every day produced acts of heroism equally conspicuous, for the attack continued with unabated force.

The sharp-shooters of the enemy were stationed thickly in the trenches; and so fatal was their aim, that for any of the garrison to be seen, only for a moment, was certain death. And, although the sentinels were changed every half-hour, nine were killed, in one day, at one post; and, after this, it was only possible to observe what the enemy were about, by some one in the force lifting up his head, and taking a momentary glance.

Early in August, the besiegers had pushed their parallels to the very edge of the fosse; but here their efforts were delayed, because the nature of the soil obliged them to bring earth from some distance to finish their works. About this time, Castellar de la Silva, at the head of fifteen hundred men, attempted to throw supplies into the city; but no precautions could escape the watchful eye of the besiegers. The convoy was seized, and only five hundred men, of the fifteen hundred who defended it, lived to tell the tale.

The main attacks of the besiegers were now directed against the ravelin, which had become the chief defence of Monjuie. Attempts were made, night after night, to storm it; but in vain. It was mined, but, as the breastwork was wholly of earth, the explosion did no injury. A battery was planted against it, and a sally was made by the besieged, hoping to destroy it. This attack was headed by a priest. He was fired upon, and fell. One of the French officers, at the risk of his own life, protected him from further injury. But his humanity cost him his life. One of the Spaniards, mistaking his object, cut him down. The guns of the battery were spiked; but this brave attack was of little use, for the French were well supplied with artillery, and fresh guns were soon mounted, and played upon the gate and ravelin.

For thirty-seven days had this fierce conflict been sustained. The numbers of the besieged were greatly reduced; the hospitals were filled to overflowing, and pestilence, with all its horrors, spread unchecked, on every side. Yet this was not all. Grim, gaunt famine was among them, and began to be severely felt. Of all their stores, only some wheat and a little flour remained. Still, there was no thought of capitulation, although every day diminished their little stock.

On the 19th of September, another general assault was made, and as bravely met. "Frequently," says Southey, "such was the press of conflict, and such the passion that inspired them, that, impatient of the time required for reloading their muskets, the defendants caught up stones from the breach, and hurled upon their enemies these readier weapons." Four times the assault was repeated in the course of two hours, and at every point the enemy was beaten off.

The noble Alvarez, during the whole assault, hastened from post to post, wherever he was most needed, providing everything, directing all, and encouraging all. Eight hundred of the besiegers fell, on this memorable day. A glorious success had been gained, yet it brought with it no rest,—no respite,—scarcely a prolongation of hope.

There was no wine to cheer the wearied soldiery, when they returned from the assault—not even bread. A scanty mess of pulse, or corn, with a little oil, or morsel of bacon, in its stead, was all that could be served out; and even this was the gift of families, who shared with the soldiers their little stores. "What matters it?" was the answer of these heroes to the lament of the inhabitants that they had nothing better to give; "if the food fail, the joy of having saved Gerona will give us strength to go on." Every day, every hour, added to the distress of the besieged. Their flour was exhausted, and, for want of other animal food, mules and horses were slaughtered, and sent to the shambles. A list was made of all within the city, and they were taken by lot. Fuel became exceedingly scarce; yet such was the patriotism of the people, that the heaps placed at the corners of the streets, to illuminate them in case of danger, remained untouched.

A glimmering of hope still remained that the city might be supplied with provisions by the army of Blake; but even this faint hope was cut off when Marshal Augereau superseded St. Cyr in the control of the siege,—for his first act was to take possession of Haslatrich, at which place Blake had stored the greater part of his magazines. Augereau sent letters to the city threatening an increase of horrors in case the siege was prolonged and offering them an armistice of a month, with provisions for that time, if Alvarez would then capitulate; but these terms were rejected with scorn. Hitherto, the few animals which had remained had been led out to feed near the burying-ground; but this was no longer possible, and the wretched animals gnawed the hair from each other's bodies. The stores of the citizens were now exhausted, and the food for the hospitals was sometimes seized on the way, by the famishing populace. Provisions were prepared in the French camp, and held out to the garrison as a temptation to desert; and yet, during the whole siege, only ten so deserted.

At length, human nature could endure no more. The chief surgeon presented to Alvarez a report on the state of the city. It was, indeed, a fearful one. It stated that "not a single house remained in a habitable state" in Gerona. The people slept in cellars, and vaults, and holes, amid the ruins; and the wounded were often killed in the hospital by the enemy's fire. The streets were broken up, so that the rain-water and sewers had stagnated, and their pestilential breath was rendered more noxious by the dead bodies which lay perishing in the ruins.

The incessant thunder of artillery had affected the atmosphere, and vegetation had stopped. The fruit withered on the trees, and nothing would grow. Within the last three days, says the report, five hundred of the garrison alone have died in the hospitals, and the pestilence is still raging unchecked. "If, by these sacrifices," say its authors, in conclusion, "deserving forever to be the admiration of history,—and if, by consummating them with the lives of us, who, by the will of Providence, have survived our comrades,—the liberty of our country can be secured, happy shall we be, in the bosom of eternity, and in the memory of all good men, and happy will be our children among their fellow-countrymen."

Alvarez himself could do no more. Yet would he not yield to the enemy; but, being seized with a delirious fever, his successor in command yielded the city on honourable terms, on the 10th of December, the siege having lasted seven months. Alvarez died soon after, and the central junta awarded honours and titles to his family, and exempted the whole city from taxation.

The surrender of this devoted city closed the campaign for 1809. The principal events of the campaign of 1810 were the battle of Busaco, in which the English gained the victory, and the retreat of the French Marshal Massena. For four months and a half, Massena had continually followed the retreating forces of Wellington, until now he had retired beyond the lines of Torres Vedras. The English had been engaged on these lines a year, until they had at last rendered them almost impregnable. They consisted of three lines of intrenchments, one within another, extending for nearly thirty miles. On these lines were a hundred and fifty redoubts, and six hundred mounted cannon. Here Massena saw his enemy retire within these lines, and he, then knew that his utmost efforts to dislodge him must prove abortive. Besides, Wellington here received reinforcements to his army, which increased it to one hundred and thirty thousand men.

Besides these defences there were twenty British ships of the line, and a hundred transports, ready to receive the army, if forced to retire. Unwilling to retreat, Massena sat down with his army here, hoping to draw Wellington to an open battle. But he preferred waiting for an attack upon his intrenchments, or to starve the enemy into a retreat. This he knew must soon be done. Wellington himself declares that Massena provisioned his sixty thousand men and twenty thousand horses, for two months, where he could not have maintained, a single division of English soldiers. But his army was now reduced to starvation; and he, driven to the last extremity, saw that he must either commence his retreat at once, or his famine-stricken army would be too weak to march. Arranging his troops into a compact mass, he placed the rear guard under the command of Ney, and retired from the Torres Vedras.

Wellington immediately commenced the pursuit; but, owing to the skilful arrangements of the French marshal, he found it impossible to attack him with success. Taking advantage of every favourable position, he would make a stand, and wait until the main body of the army had passed on, and then would himself fall back. Thus, for more than four months, did this retreat continue, until he arrived at the confines of Portugal, having lost more than one-third of his army. Many were the cruelties practised on this retreat. They have often been described, and form a dark spot on the English historian's page. All war is necessarily cruel; and the desolation and barrenness that followed in the track of the French army, wasting the inhabitants by famine, were a powerful check on Wellington in his pursuit. The track of a retreating and starving army must always be covered with woe; and one might as well complain of the cruelty of a besieging force, because innocent women and children die by hunger.

The siege of Cadiz occupied the spring and summer of this year. During this siege, a tremendous tempest ravaged the Spanish coast, lasting four days. By it more than forty sail of merchantmen, besides three line-of-battle ships, were driven on shore. It was during this tempest that the French and Swiss on board the prison-ships in the harbour made their escape.

"The storm was so great," writes one of the unhappy captives, "that we could not receive our supply of provision from the shore. Our signals of distress were wholly disregarded by the Spanish authorities; and, had it not been for the humanity of the British admiral, who sent his boats to their relief, many more of our miserable men must have perished."

The pontoons in which these prisoners were confined were not properly secured; and the prisoners on board the Castilla, seeing that the wind and tide were in their favour, cut the cable, and, hoisting a sail which they had made from their hammocks, steered for the opposite coast. They were seven hundred in number, and most of them officers. English boats were sent against them, but they found the French were prepared. The ballast of the vessel in which they were confined was cannon-balls of twenty-four and thirty-six pounds' weight. These the French hurled by hand into the boats of their pursuers, and soon disabled them, so that the fugitives finally succeeded in escaping with but little loss..

The first two months of the year 1811 were most inauspicious for the Spanish cause, General Suchet possessed himself of Tortosa, and on the 23rd of the same month Soult became master of Olivenza, On the same day died the Marquis de la Romana, one of the most skilful and noblest of the Spanish leaders; and he had scarcely expired, before his army met with a signal defeat at Gebora.

CHAPTER 4

I Fight at Barossa

Having given to my readers some slight sketches of the rise and progress of this war previous to the time when I first became an active participator in its scenes, I shall now continue it, with the history of my own adventures.

In looking back through the long series of years that have elapsed since those eventful days, there are few scenes that I can recall more vividly than that which occurred on the morning I left Gibraltar. It was my first experience of the kind, and, therefore, made a deeper impression than many after scenes, which might have been far more worthy of record than this.

It was a beautiful morning, and everywhere the troops were in motion. Horses were brought out, our baggage prepared and sent on; the light jest and laugh and joke went freely round, serving, in many instances, to conceal the thoughts that longed for utterance. Farewells were exchanged, last words spoken; and, finally, all were prepared, the word given, and our gallant little army marched out of Gibraltar. It was truly a brilliant sight; and the lively strains of our music contributed its share to make us forget that we were marching into a country at all times perilous, and now doubly so, to meet certain dangers, and, many of us, certain death.

Yet these were in the future, and lost beneath the crowd of bright and joyous anticipations that kindled in our hearts as the last loud cheering of our comrades died away, and the walls of the far-famed city receded in the distance behind our onward march. Our course was directed to Tarifa; here we had orders to wait until the forces from Cadiz should come up. An expedition had been sent out from this city, consisting of ten thousand men, three thousand of whom were British, whose object was to drive the French general out of his lines. Victor, having heard of this project, enlarged and strengthened his own forces, which now amounted to about twenty thousand men, in Andalusia.

The allied army sailed from Cadiz on the 20th of February, for Tarifa; but, a storm arising soon after they left, they were driven past this port, and disembarked at Algesiras. They marched to Tarifa on the 23rd, under the command of General Thomas Graham. Here we met; and, as we were more recently from home than these troops, we had many questions to answer, and much information both to give and receive. Before night, however, we had all our places assigned to us, and were now ready for our march. But the Spanish General La Pena had not yet arrived; and so we remained encamped here until the 27th, when he came up, with his forces; and to him General Graham, for the sake of unanimity, ceded the chief command.

All day we were busy in preparations for our morrow's march, expecting at its close to come within a short distance of the enemy's outposts. Early the next morning, our whole army was in motion. We moved forward about twelve miles, over the mountain ridges that descend from Ronda to the sea; and then, having learned that the enemy were only four leagues distance, we halted, for the purpose of reorganizing the army.

The command of the vanguard was given to Lardizabal, that of the centre to the Prince of Anglona, while General Graham had charge of the reserve, consisting of two Spanish regiments and the British troops. The cavalry of both nations, formed in one body, was commanded by Colonel Whittingham. The French army were encamped near Chiclana, narrowly observing the movements of the allied armies, and determined, at all events, to hold complete possession of the country.

The next day, March 2nd, the vanguard of our army stormed Casa Viejas. Having gained this small place, and stationed here a regiment, we continued our march on the 3rd and 4th.

Early in the morning of the 5th, as the advanced guards of our cavalry had proceeded a short distance from the main army, they suddenly came upon a squadron of French troops. Unfortunately for them, several stone fences and enclosures prevented an immediate attack, so that the French had time to form into a square, and received their charge with great coolness and intrepidity. Their square was unbroken, although numbers had fallen on both sides. A second charge was equally unsuccessful, and the colonel of our cavalry was mortally wounded. Our men then judged it most prudent to fall back upon the main army, and no attempt was made to follow them by the enemy. An anxious look-out was instituted, but the foe did not again make his appearance, and at nine o'clock the same morning our commander took up his position on the heights of Barossa.

The hill of Barossa is a low ridge, creeping in from the coast about a mile and a half, and overlooking a high broken plain. On one side of this plain rise the huge coast cliffs, while the other is skirted by the deep forest of Chiclana. Directly in front, there lies a light pine wood, beyond which rises a long narrow height, called the Bermeja. There were two ways by which this might be reached; the first was through the woods, while the second was a narrow road directly under the coast cliffs.

I have already alluded to the fact, that, although the. English and Spanish were fighting under the same banner, there was a great want of unanimity of feeling and opinion as to the course which ought to be pursued in ridding their country of their common foe. Nowhere, in the history of the war, was this more apparent than at the battle whose history I am about to relate.

The deep-seated pride of the Spanish made them unwilling to acknowledge or yield to the superiority of the British, or hardly to allow that they were at all indebted to them. A modern traveller tells us that, in a recent history of this war, which was, not long since, published in Spain, the British are not even mentioned, nor the fact of their assistance at all alluded to. It was impossible for two nations so unlike in their customs and manners, so different in language, religion, and education, to be so closely associated together as they were obliged to be, without occasions of dispute constantly occurring, which would, probably, have terminated in open rupture, had not the discipline of war prevented.

The fact that our gallant general had ceded the chief command to the weak and imperious Spanish commander had occasioned no little dissatisfaction among our men; while, from the conditions required of him by Graham, we may judge that that general himself did not pursue this course because he judged La Pena his superior in military tactics. These conditions were, that his army should make short marches; that they should be kept fresh for battle, and that they should never approach the enemy except in concentrated masses.

Although the Spanish general had pledged his word of honour that these conditions should be fulfilled, how much attention he paid to them may be judged from the fact, that, on the day but one preceding this, we had marched fifteen hours, through bad roads; and, after a short rest, had occupied the whole night in our march to Barossa. Before the troops had all arrived, or had any time for rest or refreshment, La Pena commanded the vanguard to march against San Petri, which lay about four miles distant. A detachment of the Spanish army, under Zayas, had, only two days before, commenced an intrenchment at this point; but had been surprised by the French, and driven back, so that the enemy now held possession of all the outposts down to the sea. But a short time had elapsed, after the departure of the vanguard, when we were startled by the roar of the artillery, whose rapid discharge, together with the quick volleys of musketry, showed us that a sharp engagement had already taken place. Lardizabal,—far more worthy of command than his superior,—notwithstanding the unfavourable situation in which he found himself placed, succeeded in forcing his way through the enemy's troops, leaving three hundred men dead on the field of battle, and in effecting a junction with Zayas.

Graham now endeavoured to persuade La Pena to occupy the heights of Barossa, as a superior position to the Bermeja. The Spanish general not only refused to listen to his representations, but sent an immediate order to General Graham to march through the wood to Bermeja with all the British troops. This order he obeyed, although it was in opposition to his own better judgment, leaving only two detachments at Barossa, under Major Brown, to guard the baggage. He would have left a stronger force, had he not supposed that La Pena would remain in his present position, with his own troops, and would thus assist those detachments, in case of an attack. But scarcely had the British entered the wood, when La Pena, without the least notice to his colleague, with his whole army, took the sea road under the cliffs, and marched to San Petri, leaving Barossa crowded with baggage, within sight of the enemy, and guarded only by four guns and five battalions.

No sooner did Victor, the French general, observe its defenceless state, than he advanced with a rapid pace, and, ascending behind the hill, drove off the guard, and took possession of the whole stores and provisions of our army. Major Brown, finding his force wholly inadequate to face the enemy, slowly withdrew, having immediately despatched an aid-decamp to inform General Graham of the attack. Our army had then nearly reached the Bermeja; but, as soon as the messenger arrived with the news, our general saw at once the necessity of taking the direction of affairs himself. Orders were immediately given to retrace our steps as rapidly as possible, that we might assist the Spanish army in its defence. Judge, then, of the astonishment of our general, on reaching the plain, at the view that presented itself! One side of the heights was occupied by the French, while the Spanish rear-guard was flying, with their baggage, in great confusion, on the other. On one side of us lay the cavalry of the French, and, on the other marching to the attack was a large body of troops, under Laval.

"Where is La Pena?" was the first exclamation of our commander, as, casting his eye rapidly around, he could nowhere see the least trace of him. It was impossible that he could have been defeated. The cannonade would have been heard, or at least some fugitives have taken the direction of our army. Slowly the conviction forced itself upon his mind that he had been deserted. A general burst of indignation ran along our lines; but short time was allowed for feelings like these. Only one alternative existed,—a hasty retreat, or an immediate attack. It need hardly be said that Graham chose the latter.

Ten guns immediately opened their fire upon Laval's troops, and were promptly answered back by the artillery of the French. No time was given to the British to form with any attention to regiments; but, hastily dividing themselves into two masses, they rushed to the attack. The charge on the left was, indeed, a furious one, for we felt that conquest or death was the alternative. It was bravely met, however, on the part of the French. After the first discharge of artillery, the soldiers pressed rapidly onward, and were soon mingled with the foe in fierce and deadly conflict. The front ranks of the French were pressed back upon the second line, which, unable to withstand the shock, was broken in the same manner, and scattered in much confusion, only the chosen battalion remaining to cover the retreat.

Ruffin, who commanded the enemy on the right, had stationed his troops just within the wood, where they awaited, in perfect order, the division under Brown, who rushed with headlong haste to the contest. When they had nearly readied the wood, they discharged their musketry. Nearly half of Brown's detachment fell at the first fire; yet, nothing daunted, the remainder maintained their ground, until another detachment came to their aid. Then, mingling close in the dreadful combat, they pressed together to the brow of the hill, without either party gaining a decided advantage. Here the contest continued, with more bravery than before. The issue still remained quite doubtful, when the British, retiring a short distance, again rushed to the attack. Ruffin and Rousseau, the French leaders, both fell, mortally wounded, and the French were obliged to retire, leaving three of their guns in possession of their enemies.

Discomfited but not disheartened, they withdrew again, re-formed, and rushed to the attack. But they found no slumbering foe. Our guns were well manned. Their fire was reserved until the enemy were close at hand, and then they were allowed to tell upon that living mass. The execution was terrible. Closely and rapidly, discharge followed discharge. Again and again were they summoned to the attack; but the lines had hardly closed over their dying comrades, when another volley would again send confusion and death among the advancing ranks. Victor saw it was useless to struggle longer. The trumpet sounded, the contest stopped, and in less than an hour the English were again undisputed masters of Barossa.

And where, during this conflict, were the Spanish troops, in whose cause the British were so freely lavishing, not only treasure, but their own lives? Scarcely three miles away, the report of every round of musketry reached La Pena's ears. He knew that his ally was placed under great disadvantages; yet he could look idly on, not knowing, scarcely caring, apparently, how the contest should be decided. In vain did many of his brave troops mount their chargers, and wait only for the word of command to rush upon the enemy. He listened neither to the voice of honour nor to the entreaties of his officers, nor to the ill-repressed murmurings of the soldiery.

No stroke in aid of the British was struck by a Spanish sabre that day; although one or two regiments, unable longer to contain their indignation, left without orders, and came up in season to witness the defeat of the French. And thus terminated the attack on Barossa. Scarcely two hours had passed from the first alarm before the French were retreating beyond our reach, for our troops were too much exhausted by their twenty-two hours' march, and their still longer fast, to think of pursuing.

Yet, short as the conflict was, the terrible evidences of its fatality lay all around us. Fifty officers, sixty sergeants, and more than eleven hundred British soldiers, had fallen, while two thousand of the enemy were either killed or wounded. Six guns, an eagle, two generals mortally wounded, and four hundred prisoners, fell into the power of the English. La Pena's conduct during this battle was complained of by our commander, and the Spanish *cortes* went through the forms of arresting him; but he was soon after released, without investigation, and published what he called his justification, in which he blamed Graham severely for his disobedience of orders.

When the last of the enemy had disappeared in the distance, the troops were all summoned to the field of battle. We collected there, and gazed around with saddened hearts. Four hours ago, and there was not one, of all that now lay lifeless on that bloody field, whose heart did not beat as high as our own, whose hopes were not as brilliant; and yet, their sun had now set forever! I know of no sadder scene than a field of battle presents soon after the conflict, even though the glorious result may have filled our hearts with joy. When the roll is called, and name after name uttered without response, it cannot but awaken the deepest sensibility in the heart of the survivors. And then the hasty burial of the dead, and the hurried sending off the wounded, the surgeon's necessary operations, and the groans of the sufferers, all make us feel that these are the horrors of war.

Before the battle is the rapid marching and counter-marching, and the enlivening strains of martial music, the encouraging words of the officers,—more than all, the excitement which must exist in such a scene,—and all these serve to elevate and sustain the spirits. During the contest the excitement increases, until all sense of fear and danger is lost. But one thing is seen—the foe;—but one object exists—to conquer.

When all these have passed away, and there is no longer aught to excite, then the eye opens on stern and dread reality, and we realize what we have escaped, and the pain and suffering ever attendant on such scenes. There is something awfully trying to the soul, when the last sad rites are being performed for those so lately buoyant in life and health,— especially when we meet with the corpses of those we have known and loved. I have seen many affecting instances of such recognitions. Among others that I might name, is that of a French captain of dragoons, who came over after the battle with a trumpet, and requested permission to search among the dead for his colonel. His regiment was a fine one, with bright brass helmets and black horse-hair, bearing a strong resemblance to the costume of the ancient Romans. Many of our own soldiers accompanied him in his melancholy search.

It was long before we found the French colonel, for he was lying on his face, his naked body weltering in blood. As soon as he was turned over, the captain recognized him. He uttered a sort of agonizing scream, sprang off his horse, dashed his helmet on the ground, knelt by the body, and, taking the bloody hand in his own, kissed it many times, in an agony of grief. He seemed entirely to forget, in his sorrow, that any one was present.

We afterwards learned that the colonel had, in his youth, done him a great service, by releasing him from the police when evil company had led him to the commission of some crime. It was his first act of the kind; and gratitude to the colonel led to an immediate enlistment in his corps. From that hour he had been to the captain as a father, and it was through his influence that he had attained his present rank in the army. The scene was truly an affecting one; and it was with feelings of deep sympathy that we assisted him in committing the body to the earth.

Our gallant commander remained on the field of battle all that day; and when all the last sad duties were performed, and as many of the commissariat mules as could be found were gathered in, we marched from the scene of our late victory, and took up our position behind the Isla. The news of our victory was received in England with much joy, and our own regiment, the 28th, was spoken of with peculiar honour. These contests in Spain called forth much newspaper praise, and awakened the lyre of many a poet in the halls of old England. Perhaps the following lines from Southey, written on this battle, may be acceptable to the reader:

Though the four quarters of the world have seen
The British valour proved triumphantly
Upon the French, in many a field far famed,
Yet may the noble island in her rolls
Of glory write Barossa's name. For there
Not by the issue of deliberate plans,
Consulted well, was the fierce conflict won,—
Nor by the leader's eye intuitive,
Nor force of either arm of war, nor art
Of skilled artillerist, nor the discipline
Of troops to absolute obedience trained,—
But by the spring and impulse of the heart,
Brought fairly to the trial, when all else
Seemed like a wrestler's garment thrown aside,
By individual courage, and the sense
Of honour, their old country's and their own,
There to be forfeited, or there upheld,—
This warmed the soldier's soul, and gave his hand
The strength that carries with it victory.
More to enhance their praise, the day was fought
Against all circumstance; a painful march
Through twenty hours of night and day prolonged
Forespent the British troops, and hope delayed
Had left their spirits palled. But when the word
Was given to turn, and charge, and win the heights,
The welcome order came to them like rain
Upon a traveller in the thirsty sands.
Rejoicing, up the ascent, and in the front
Of danger, they with steady step advanced,

And with the insupportable bayonet
Drove down the foe. The vanquished victor saw,
And thought of Talavera, and deplored
His eagle lost. But England saw, well pleased,
Her old ascendency that day sustained;
And Scotland, shouting over all her hills,
Among her worthies ranked another Graham.

The brilliant success gained on the heights of Barossa was but the prelude of other victories. The star of Napoleon, so long in the ascendant, had begun to decline in the horizon. Obliged to draw off many of his troops, those that remained felt the want of his guiding hand. Division reigned in the councils of his generals; and the British leader, ever ready to take advantage, and ever on the watch for opportunity, saw his favourable moment, and followed it up.

CHAPTER 5

My Time on the March

The French had retreated from Portugal, followed at every step by the army of the English. After the battle of Barossa, Graham had withdrawn from the command of our army, and joined that of Wellington, while Sir Thomas Picton took his place.

We remained for a number of days near our position, while these changes were taking place, and then orders arrived that we should proceed at once to the mountains of the Sierra Morena, to assist in harassing the retreat of the French. We had scarcely commenced our march when our provisions began to fail, owing to the conduct of the Portuguese government, who would not supply their troops with provisions; and so they were unable to continue the pursuit, while numbers were perishing for want of food. Our generals could not see their allies suffering thus, and our own supplies were shared with them, and we were all put upon short allowance.

Half a pound of bread, and half a pound of salt pork, was all that we received for a day's provision. And we were ascending mountains covered with woods and deep forests, infested by guerrillas, who often fell upon and murdered our men, if they strayed away from the ranks. To prevent this was impossible; for, if there were provisions in the country, men in our starving condition would not fail to obtain them; but scarcely anything could be found, at this season.

The French army were also suffering for want of food, and, as they preceded us in their retreat, they either devoured or destroyed everything that could sustain life. The poor peasants on their route fled from their homes, and shrunk equally from French and English, for they well knew that either would equally deprive them of the little they possessed. The sufferings of the peasantry were truly terrible.

In the third day of our march, a scene occurred which I shall never forget. We were slowly toiling up a huge mountain, so exhausted, from fatigue and want, that we could hardly proceed. When about half-way to the summit, we perceived before us a large house. Some of our men hastened to it at once, hoping to procure some provision. The slight fastenings of the door soon yielded to their eager haste, and they were about to rush in, when their steps were arrested by the misery the scene presented. The floor was covered with persons in a state of actual starvation. Thirty women and children had already expired; and, scattered around among the corpses, lay fifteen or sixteen more wretched beings, still breathing, but unable to speak.

Hungry as we were, the hearts of the soldiers were moved at the scene, and our next day's provision was cheerfully contributed to rescue them from death. But this kindness could only delay their fate. They were too weak to seek for more food; they had scarcely strength to eat the little we could offer them; and it is more than probable that every one perished.

The next day my comrade, who had been fast failing, declared himself unable to proceed. He was a fine fellow,—one that I had known in Ireland, and to whom I was much attached. Feeble as we were, we could not leave him behind, and we carried him a short distance; but he soon died. Permission was given us to carry him a little way from the camp to bury him. We hollowed out a shallow grave, wrapped him in his blanket, and left him to his fate.

Near the spot where we interred him was a small house, which we entered, and were fortunate enough to obtain a little wine. While in the house, we heard a scream, as of fear. We hastened out, and saw several of our soldiers running swiftly towards the camp, from the place where we had interred our comrade. They had dug him up, for the purpose of robbing him of his blanket. As they were ripping it open, the knife entered the flesh, and he began to struggle. It was this that had so frightened them. We went to the poor fellow, finished removing his blanket, and found that he was still alive. Want and fatigue had produced a state of insensibility resembling death, from which he had been aroused by the pain of his wound. We shared with him the little wine we had obtained, which so revived him that he was able to accompany us back from his own funeral. He soon after recovered, and returned home to Ireland.

A day or two after this occurrence, I left the company, with one of my companions, and went higher up the mountain, in search of wild pigs, which are sometimes found there. This was absolutely against our orders; but, as we were literally starving to death, the consequences of disobedience, and the dangers of our journey, weighed but little in the balance. I agreed to search one side of the mountain, while he ascended the other, and we were to meet at the top. When about half-way up the mountain, I was stopped by a ball whizzing close past my ear. Thinking that it might be my comrade, who did not see me, I turned, and, looking around, soon saw the green feather of my assailant, projecting over a rock. At this I was somewhat alarmed; for he was so completely hid behind the rock that I could not fire at him, and I knew that he was reloading his musket. In a moment more he fired again, but, fortunately for me, his musket flashed in the pan. There was still only his feather in sight; at this I fired, and struck it. I then reloaded as hastily as possible, and advanced cautiously up the mountain, hoping to get sight of him.

As I was coming round the point of the rock, he sprang forward, laid down his gun, spread out his arms, and exposed himself to my shot. I knew, by his motions, that he had no ammunition, and as I had no desire to kill him, I fixed my bayonet on my gun, as if I would make a charge, and then advanced towards him, in a friendly manner. But, when I was within twice the length of my gun from him, he picked up his musket and attacked me. Darting back to avoid his bayonet, I fired my own gun, and he fell to the ground. I examined his knapsack, and found that it bore the mark of the 95th rifle brigade of our own division. He was a guerrilla, and had doubtless killed the man whose knapsack he bore. I examined his canteen, and found, to my great surprise, a pint of Jamaica brandy. In my exhausted state, this was a discovery which gave me the greatest pleasure. I took some of it, and, feeling quite refreshed, pursued my search for game.

I had not gone far before I discovered a small pig, which I succeeded in shooting. This I carried with me to the top of the mountain, where I found my comrade awaiting me. He had been less successful than myself, having found nothing. He asked me how I had fared. I told him that I had shot an old hog and a little pig, at which he expressed great pleasure. I then showed him the contents of the canteen, which he joyfully shared with me; and, having related my adventure, we retraced our steps to the camp. We concealed our treasure as well as we were able; but, notwithstanding all our care, the first person we saw, on our return, was the adjutant. He came up to us, and demanded where we had been. Upon the mountain, in search of food, was my reply. He told me, if he should report us, as he was required to do, we should be shot for disobeying orders. I answered, that it made little difference with us; it would only hasten affairs, as it was impossible to survive much longer without food. "Did you find any?" he asked. We showed him our prize. He would gladly have purchased it of us; but food, in our condition, was far more precious than money, and we refused his offer of a doubloon, with the assurance that five would be no temptation to part with it. But, on arrival at our quarters, as we were cutting up the pig, gratitude for his kindness, in not reporting us, so far overcame our selfishness, that we sent him a quarter of it. The remainder made our mess a fine meal; and we certainly were never in a better condition to estimate the value of food than when we devoured the little pig of the Morena.

CHAPTER 6

Guerrillas

I have alluded to the annoyance by guerrillas, or, as they were sometimes called, *Partidas*. These were principally, at first, Spanish peasants, who, unable to present any efficient force against the French, and unwilling to submit to them, threw themselves into the mountains, and, being well acquainted with all the passes and hiding-places, did the French much damage, by cutting off their communications, robbing their stores, and murdering every one who dared to stray from the main army. As the war proceeded, their numbers were enlarged by all those who were weary of the restraints of law;—every robber that feared a jail, or could break from one; every smuggler whose trade had been interrupted,—and there were thousands of these, as there still are, in Spain; every one who was weary of the restraints of his life, and sought for excitement; and all idlers who preferred the wild and reckless daring of these troops to the drill and watch of the army, were found either as associate or chief in these bands.

They soon became regularly organized, chose their chiefs, and had watchwords, by which they could obtain a safe pass all over the country. They were professedly our allies, but they were almost as much a terror to us as to our foes. They proved, however, invaluable to our army, as a means of communication with each other, and as spies on the movements of our enemies. It was impossible for the French to communicate with each other at all, except by sending strong escorts, and these were often cut off; while, on our side, news could be sent with almost the rapidity of telegraph, and this undoubtedly was a great advantage to us. The chiefs of these bands were often obliged to procure subsistence and treasure for themselves, by robbing their own countrymen; and, indeed, one of the principal causes of the sudden growth of these bands was the hope of intercepting the public and private plate, which was being carried from all parts of Spain to be coined into money. Yet, though most of the bands were worthless characters, there were some among them of more noble spirit. Some were actuated by revenge—some by a gallant, enterprising spirit—and a few by an honest ambition to serve their country.

Our troops often met with many adventures with these foes; and many were the weary hours, in our toilsome marches, that were beguiled by the recital of their hair-breadth escapes, or their own wonderful adventures. Some of these were of so much interest that I cannot refrain from a desire to recount a few to my readers.

Don Julian Sanchez was the son of a farmer, on the banks of the Guebra. The little cottage where he resided, with his parents and one sister, was the abode of happiness and plenty. In an evil hour, the French army passed that way. Their cattle were driven away and slaughtered, and their little harvest, just reaped, became the prey of the plunderers. Terrified and despairing, Julian fled, with his parents and sister, to the woods. But his parents were old, and, before they could reach the shelter of the wood, they were overtaken, carried back to the cottage, and murdered, in cold blood, on their own hearthstone. Julian and his sister concealed themselves in a cave; but the next day he left her there, and went to see if he could obtain any trace of his parents.

Directing his course to their little cottage, he found their murdered corpses. Revenge and anger, in a spirit like Julian's, was deep, not loud. He shed no tear, uttered no complaint,—but calmly proceeded to inter the bodies of his parents in a humble grave. Then, kneeling on the sod, he swore revenge on their murderers,—a revenge which should be followed till his latest breath. He returned to his sister; but, as he approached the cave where he had left her, what a sight met his view! A party of the hated army were just issuing from its precincts. The body of his beautiful sister lay on the ground naked,—dishonoured,—the victim of a vile outrage.

Julian gazed for a moment on the scene. He had no time for tears, and he had sworn to live for revenge,—a vow which now burned itself in deeper characters upon his soul. He turned away. A huge rock overhung the cave. He ascended it, and, secreting himself in a little fissure where he could be heard, not seen, he gazed for a few moments on the chief of the band, till every line of his countenance was impressed on his soul. Then, calling to him from the rock, he said, "You hear me, but you see me not. I am a Spaniard, the son of those parents you murdered yesterday—the brother of her whose corpse lies before you. You are their murderer; and I swear, by the Holy Virgin, that I will never lose sight for one day of your path, until my hands are imbrued in your heart's best blood! You may think to escape me; but remember, you shall die by my hand!"

In a moment, the troops of the French were on the rock. They searched everywhere for the speaker, but no trace of him could be found, until, just as they had relinquished their search, one of the number fell dead by the blow of an unseen assassin. He was the first of the band that fell. Months passed away. Julian had never since met his foe; but the frequent death of his followers, and the daring exploits of robbery that were constantly performing in his camp, often called to mind the voice he had heard. A few months after, in battle, this officer was attacked, and would have been killed, had not a Spaniard saved his life, at the risk of his own. He turned to thank his unknown deliverer, but was met with so fierce a look of hate, that he involuntarily shrunk from it. "I desire no thanks," said the Spaniard; "your life is mine, and none but me shall take it."

The voice was recognized, but its owner had glided away in the confusion. A year had elapsed, when this officer was again sent to the banks of the Guebra, and took up his quarters in the very house Julian's father formerly occupied. The first night of his stop there was enlivened by the arrival of four of the same party who had met with him the year before. In joyous mood, they had seated themselves around the table, and were discussing the events of the campaign. Suddenly they were startled by a deep voice, which the officer had cause to remember, and Julian, with four of his associates, glided into the room.

So sudden, so unexpected, was the attack, that they had not time to grasp their swords, ere they were pinioned and led away. Julian and the chief alone remained. "Look at me," said Julian; "do you know me? In this very room, a year ago, my parents fell by your murderous hand. The stain of their blood still remains to witness against you. In that wood lies the corpse of my idolized and only sister. You were her assassin. You heard my vow. Not for one day have I left your steps. Twice have I warded death from your head; but when I saw you desecrate again this hearthstone by your accursed presence, I knew that your time had come. Frenchman, prepare to die!"

After the death of this man, Julian succeeded in organizing a regular band. At the head of these, he would again and again assault the enemy, even though they outnumbered his own band many times. Another instance of his daring intrepidity, at a time when we were suffering for want of provisions, and of the patience with which he followed up his designs, deserves to be recorded. It was the custom of the French garrison to send out their cattle beyond the walls every morning, for the purpose of grazing, under the protection of a guard, which at once kept them from wandering too far, and also watched the movements of the Spanish army. Don Julian determined, if possible, to surprise the herd. For this purpose, he concealed himself, with his band, day after day, among the broken ground, near the river. But the guard was still too powerful and vigilant to allow him to make the attempt.

At length, as if to reward him for his patience, fortune threw in his way, not only the object for which he sought, but one of far more importance to him. On a certain day, the governor of the place where the garrison was stationed came out, accompanied by a very slender escort, and ventured imprudently to cross the river, at the self-same spot where Julian lay concealed. He was instantly surrounded, and made prisoner. Almost at the same moment, the cattle, frightened by the explosion of a shell which fell among them, ran towards the river. The guard followed, but overtook them at such a distance from the city, that Julian thought himself justified in making the attack. It was attended with perfect success and governor and cattle were conveyed in triumph to the British headquarters.

Another of these chiefs was named Juan Martin Diaz, or the Empecinado. When the news of the detention of Ferdinand at Bayonne first reached Spain, he was engaged as a farmer. Young, ardent, and daring, he threw aside his plough, and persuaded a neighbouring youth, only sixteen, to join him. Their first object was to procure horses and arms. They took post upon the high road from France to Madrid, for the purpose of intercepting the French couriers. An occasion soon occurred.

A party of six men were riding past a narrow defile. An old woman went out and arrested the progress of the last two, by offering them some fruit for sale. She detained them until the others were in advance some distance; then the two youths fired from their covert, and their victims fell. Long before the others returned for their comrades, their horses and arms were far away. These boys were soon joined by others, of which Juan was the chief; and, as he grew older and had more experience, his band increased, until it numbered one thousand five hundred men. With these he performed the most daring exploits, cutting off supplies, and intercepting convoys.

By his intelligence, activity, and bravery, he was enabled to do the enemy much mischief. In vain were armies sent to surround his band. They concealed themselves in their fastnesses, and baffled them all, until his very name became a terror to the French armies. He gave no quarter to the conquered; and such was his discipline of his followers, and his generosity in the division of the spoils, that he became the idol of his band, and they were willing to undertake any exploit at his bidding.

A convoy was conveying, in a carriage, a lady, a relative of Marshal Moncey. The coach was escorted by twelve soldiers, in the centre of two columns of six thousand each, about a mile asunder. The Empecinado, with only eight of his followers, was concealed close to the town of Caraveas. He allowed the leading column to pass, then boldly rushed upon the convoy, put to death the whole of the escort, seized and carried off the carriage; and, when the alarm was given, Martin and his prize were in safety in the mountains, where he effectually eluded the search made after him. He saved the life of the lady, who was sent to his own house, and had every attention paid her. This convoy was a very rich prize of money and jewels. This he divided among his men, reserving only a small share for himself.

He often met with very narrow escapes. On one occasion, he was unhorsed and disarmed, and the sword of his opponent passed through his arm, and entered his side. His wound seemed to give him a new courage. He suddenly sprang at his foe, and, seizing him by the neck, dragged him to the ground. He fell with him, however, but continued to keep uppermost. The other refusing to surrender, the Empecinado held him fast with one hand, while with the other he snatched up a stone, and beat him to death. On another occasion, he was nearly made prisoner by some Spanish troops in the pay of the French; and, finding every other hope of escape impossible, he threw himself down an immense precipice, rather than fall into their hands. His fall was broken by the projecting limbs of trees, covered with very thick foliage. He was discovered here by one of his followers, and taken home. He recovered finally, after suffering a severe illness, which for some time prevented his taking the field.

The most distinguished of these courageous leaders was Xavier Mina. He was a student at Pamplona when the revolution broke out. His father was a considerable land-owner, and deputy for one of the valleys of Navarre. Some act of injustice, practised towards his father, had driven young Xavier to desperation. His resolution was taken. He threw aside his studies, went to his native village, and, summoning around him the young men of his acquaintance, related his wrongs, and urged them to join him in his career of revenge. Moved by his enthusiastic address, twelve of his companions volunteered to join him. Arming themselves with muskets and ammunition, they sought the mountain passes, and maintained themselves, while awaiting opportunities of action, by subsisting on the sheep belonging to Mina's father.

His first adventure was to surprise a party of seven artillery-men, who were carrying two pieces of cannon and a quantity of ammunition from Saragossa to Pamplona. When the news of this success reached his village, others were encouraged to volunteer. His next exploit was, with his band of twenty, to attack a general officer, who was escorted by twenty-four foot and twelve horsemen. Stationing his men in a narrow defile, he gave orders to fire as they were descending, each one having selected his man. Twenty of the escort were thus levelled to the earth, before they had any intimation of their danger. The general was one of the number. The rest of the escort were made prisoners, and a large sum of money fell into Mina's hands. This he distributed among his men, advising them to send part to their families, and retain no more than would suffice for the expenses of their own interment, exposed as they now continually were to death.

The men were thus raised in their own estimation, and in that of their countrymen, wherever this was told; and volunteers soon presented themselves in abundance, attracted by a success which was reported everywhere with the usual exaggerations. He received, however, only such persons as he regarded as a valuable acquisition to his band. These wore a red ribbon in their hats, and a red collar to their jackets.

In Arragon, a band of fifty robbers were adding to the miseries of that unhappy country. Having heard of their atrocities, Mina turned his course thither. He succeeded in surprising them. The greater part were killed on the spot, and the remainder sent as prisoners to Tarragona. Rations were voluntarily raised for his people, wherever they were expected, and given as freely at one time as they were paid for at another by the spoils of the enemy. It was in vain that the French made repeated efforts to crush this enterprising enemy. If his band were dispersed, it was only to unite, and, by striking a blow in some weak point, render themselves more formidable than before.

A large number of prisoners, and an amount of treasure, were to be sent from Vittoria to France. Twelve hundred men accompanied it as an escort. At the Puerto de Arlaban, they were attacked by the seemingly omnipresent Mina, of whose absence, in another part of the country, they thought themselves assured. They were entirely routed; but, unfortunately, two hundred of the prisoners were slain in the contest. Information of the journey of this escort had been procured from a new recruit in Mina's band, who had his own object to accomplish by it. He was a gentleman of some standing, who was engaged to a beautiful Spanish lady. Her affections had been stolen from him by a wounded French officer, quartered in her father's house. He had recovered, and was now taking his bride home to France. The former lover had sworn a deep revenge, and, unable himself to accomplish this object, had enlisted the powerful Mina on his side.

When the band returned to their haunts, they carried with them six ladies, who were guilty of the same crime, *viz.*, having accepted, as husbands, French officers. Their fate was, indeed, a sad one. The contest for them had been fierce in the extreme. They had seen their protectors, one by one, fall around them, fighting until the last breath in their defence; and now they were left helpless to the mercy of their conquerors. A mock trial was instituted. They were found guilty of aiding the enemies of their country, and all of them executed.

But Mina was not always successful. Not long after this, he had attacked and overcome a party of French. As he was conveying his prisoners to Robres, he was betrayed by one of his own men, and was attacked as suddenly as he had fallen upon others. His band were scattered, many of them slain, and he escaped, with great difficulty, with his own life. One week afterward, he appeared in the Rioja, with five thousand men, and attacked a Polish regiment, which was retiring to France. They were entirely routed.

Mina enlarged his band by an accession of every one of the Spanish prisoners whom he had liberated, and filled his coffers with the booty. One million of francs fell into his hands, besides the equipages, arms and stores of all kinds, and a quantity of church plate. Two weeks after, he captured another convoy, going from Valencia to France. General Abbé now bent his whole force to disperse his troops. For three days in succession he followed Mina's troops to their haunts, and each day defeated them; so that, on the last day, Mina was obliged again to flee alone for his life. Yet, not discouraged, he struggled on with various success, until at length he fell into the hands of the French, who sent him a prisoner to France.

Great rejoicings were made when the capture of this formidable enemy was reported; but they soon found that they had little reason for joy, for his place at the head of the band was taken by his uncle, Francisco, who proved himself, if possible, even more formidable than his nephew. His various adventures would well fill a volume, and it is easy to see the interest they must have possessed when related around the bivouac fire on those mountains, where no one knew but that any moment might bring his army around them.

CHAPTER 7

I March to Badajoz

But to return to my own history.

We were still pursuing our weary course, sometimes coming within sight of our enemies, and sometimes marching and counter-marching, when our leaders thought best to avoid a battle. We were still suffering the pangs of hunger, our principal food being a supply of ground bark. The soldiers continued to wander away, and often escaped, with their lives, from imminent peril.

One of our men observed, at a little distance from the camp, a commotion in the bushes, which he thought was occasioned by some wild animal; and he hastened out to secure it. Creeping cautiously along under the bushes, his course was suddenly arrested by a bullet flying over him. Having passed around a rock which concealed him from the camp, he hastily jumped up, and looked round. He soon spied a woman sitting near a small spring, with a child in her arms, as he thought; but, concluding that it was best to be on his guard, he crept cautiously near her, and soon saw that she was thoroughly armed, and what seemed to be a child was something which certainly did not possess life. The shot had evidently been fired by her, and she was watching for his reappearance. He fired, and killed her. On taking her arms, he discovered that it was one of the guerrillas, dressed in female apparel, and evidently intended for a decoy. Judging from articles found around him, all our troops had not been so successful as was our soldier in discovering the disguise.

There are not many villages on these mountains, and but few scattered habitations. The next day after the adventure I have just related, a small party of us again left in search of food. We soon found, in a beautiful valley, a small house. We knocked for admission. There was no answer; so, without further ceremony, the door was broken down, and we entered. A fire was found burning on the hearth, showing, however desolate the hut might now be, it had not long wanted inhabitants. We found, however, no food, and were turning away, quite disappointed, when one of our number spied an open hole in the garden. We found there, to our great delight, two pigs of wine, which our near approach had probably disturbed its owners in their attempts to conceal.

These pig-skins were to us quite a curiosity. The skin is taken as entire as possible from the animal, and turned so that the hair will be inside, and then preserved in such a way as to make it capable of holding wine. These are the common wine-casks of the country. I have often seen loads of them; and so perfectly do they retain their resemblance, that any one unaccustomed to the sight would say, at once, that they were loads of dead porkers. We took our wine, and returned as rapidly as possible to the lines, to share our good fortune with our comrades.

A day or two after this, as we were encamped on one of the hills which overlooked the country to a great distance, a movement on the plains below attracted the attention of our officers. Scouts were instantly sent out, to learn the nature of it. Animation again appeared in the faces of our men; for, even if it were the enemy, we all felt it would be far better to win an honourable death in an open battle, than to perish daily, as we were doing, by hunger and murder.

It was not long before our messengers returned, spurring their horses, and joy in every feature of their countenances. As soon as they came within hearing, they flung up their caps in the air, shouting, "Relief, relief! Our commissariat is coming! It will soon be here!" The excitement among our men was intense. They could hardly be restrained from rushing down immediately to break upon the long-expected, long-delayed supplies.

When, at length, they came near, and we saw the baggage-wagons, accompanied by a strong escort, the ill-repressed enthusiasm of the men burst forth in one long, deafening shout, that reverberated from the tops of those mountains for miles around. The scene then presented by our camp was, indeed, an exciting one. Officers were engaged on all sides in distributing provisions to the starving troops, and these in administering cordials and refreshments to their sick comrades. Many of the sick, who were apparently near their end, revived and soon recovered.

The same escort brought information that the destination of Wellington's army was now to be changed, and our division of it was directed to proceed immediately to Badajos. This, too, was joyful news; and, with the morrow's dawn, everything was ready for motion. Tents were struck, our baggage stored, and order everywhere restored. Once more we had an aim, an object; and, with this, it was easy to become again docile and obedient. I shall never forget the sensation of pleasure that throbbed in our hearts, as our last column denied down the mountain, and we bade farewell to those haunts, which had been so nearly fatal to us all. Our course was immediately directed to Badajos, and, on the 3rd of May, we sat down three leagues from its walls.

CHAPTER 8

The Siege of Badajoz

Badajos, the capital of the Spanish province of Estremadura, is situated near the Portuguese frontier, at the confluence of the small stream of the Rivillas with the Guadiana. It is very strongly fortified, both nature and art having contributed their stores to render its position impregnable. A huge rock, one hundred feet high, overlooks the meeting of the waters. On the top of this rock rises an old castle, venerable from its age, and itself a strong fortification.

The town occupies a triangular space between the rivers, and is protected by eight curtains and bastions, from twenty-three to thirty feet high, with good counterscarps, covered way and glacis. On the left bank of the Guadiana there is a *lunette*, covering a dam and sluice, which commands an inundation. Beyond the Rivillas stands an isolated redoubt, called the Picurina. This is four hundred yards from the town. Two hundred yards from the ramparts, rises a defective crown-work, called the Pardaleras. On the right bank of the Guadiana rises a hill, crowned by a regular fort, three hundred feet square, called San Christoval. A bridge, supported by twenty-two stone arches, crosses the stream, and this is protected by a bridge head.

The strength of this place made its possession a desirable object to both parties. It had been early invested by the French, under Soult, and vigorously assaulted. It was, however, well defended, and would probably have maintained its position, had it not been for the weakness and inefficiency of its commanding officers, which caused the battle of the Gebora to terminate in a shameful defeat and immense loss to the Spanish army.

Rafael Menacho was next made commander of the place. He sustained the siege with great spirit, and everything seemed to promise favourably, when Menacho was unfortunately killed, during a sally, and the command devolved upon Imas, a man most unfitted for this situation. He surrendered, almost without a struggle, to the French; although he had received certain information that a strong army was moving to his assistance, and would soon raise the siege. He demanded that his grenadiers should march out of the breach. Permission was granted, but they were obliged themselves to enlarge it, before they could do so.

The French immediately took possession of the city, and strengthened its defences. Lord Wellington was much chagrined at the loss of this place, and early in May sent Lord William Stewart to invest it. The siege was carried on with vigour, but under great disadvantages, arising from want of the proper materials for construction of the works. In endeavouring to erect their batteries, the engineers were obliged to labour exposed to a heavy fire from the city, which proved so destructive, that, before one small battery against one of the outworks of the town was completed, seven hundred men and five officers had fallen. When, at length, on the morning of the 11th of May, this battery was completed, before night five of its guns were silenced by the enemy, and the rest were so exposed that it was impossible to man them.

The same day news reached our army that the French army were coming to the relief of Badajos. Immediately our commander took steps to raise the siege, as to remain there would have exposed our whole force to destruction. On the night of the 13th, he removed all his artillery and platforms; and on that of the 14th, his guns and stores. But so secretly was this done, that the French were entirely ignorant of it, until, as the rear guard were about being drawn off, they made a sally, and, of course, discovered it. Soon after this, the battle of Albuera occurred.

Our own division was not, however, engaged in this battle, having been ordered to Campo Mayor, where, on the 24th, orders reached us that we were again to march for Badajos, Lord Wellington having resolved to invest it in person. We immediately marched, and arrived on the evening of the 27th, where we found Lord Wellington, with ten thousand men. During the absence of our army, Phillipon, the governor of the place, had entirely destroyed the little remains of fortifications left by them, repaired all his own damages, and procured a fresh supply of wine and vegetables from the country. He had also mounted more guns, and interested the towns-people on his side.

The works of the siege were commenced under Wellington's own direction, on the 29th, and carried on a week, with various success. Then it was resolved to make an assault upon Fort Christoval. The storming party, preceded by a forlorn hope, and led by Major McIntosh, with the engineer Forster as a guide, reached the glacis and descended to the ditch about midnight, on the night of the sixth of June. The French had, however, cleared all the rubbish away, so that seven feet perpendicular still remained; and above this were many obstacles, such as carts chained together, pointed beams of wood, and large shells ranged along the ramparts, to roll down upon the assailants.

The forlorn hope, finding that the breach was still impracticable, was retiring, with little loss, when they met the main body, leaping into the ditch with ladders, and the ascent was again attempted; font the ladders were too short, and the confusion and mischief occasioned by the bursting of the shells was so great that the assailants again retired, with the loss of more than one hundred men.

Two nights after, a second attack was made, but met with no better success.

The British troops, with loud shouts, jumped into the ditch. The French defied them to come on, and at the same time rolled barrels of powder and shells down, while the musketry made fearful and rapid havoc. In a little time, the two leading columns united at the main breach; the supports also came up; confusion arose about the ladders, of which only a few could be reared; and the enemy, standing on the ramparts, bayoneted the foremost assailants, overturned the ladders, and again poured their destructive fire upon the crowd below. One hundred and forty men had already fallen, and yet not a single foot had been gained, nor was there one bright spot in the darkness to encourage them to proceed. The order was given to retire.

The next day, Wellington heard that the army of Soult was again advancing to attack him; and as to receive battle there would throw all the disadvantage on his side, he thought best to raise the siege. On the 10th, the stores were all removed, and the siege turned to a blockade, which was afterwards terminated, when the armies of Marmont and Soult, having effected a junction, advanced to its relief. It was nearly a year before the allied army again found it desirable to approach Badajos. Meanwhile the war was carried on with great activity, although with varied success.

My own time was passed with the regiment to which I belonged, either in the mountains, or in foraging or bringing supplies, as circumstances dictated.

Although again and again engaged in light skirmishes with small bodies of the enemy, occupied as our own regiment were, it was not my fortune to engage in a general battle, until the last siege of Badajos. And as this city was one of the most important, and its siege the best sustained of any on the Peninsula, I shall give an account of it more in detail than I have thought best to do of the rest.

The unfavourable issue of the two former investments, had induced Lord Wellington to wait until a combination of favourable circumstances should at least give more hope of success. The auspicious moment had, in his view, now arrived. The heavy rains which occur at this season of the year would so raise the rivers in the high lands, where his troops were located, that there would be no risk of their detention in proceeding at once to the Alemtejo, while this same flow of waters, in the more level portion occupied by the French, would prove a fatal impediment to the junction of their forces, which were at this time considerably scattered, owing to the difficulty of obtaining provisions. Regiments were despatched, therefore, to bring all the stores of clothing and provisions from the different points where they had been left, and concentrate them near Badajos.

Wellington himself, having remained at his headquarters, on the Coa, until the last moment, in order to conceal his real intentions, now came in person to superintend the new works. As the French had strongly occupied the stone bridge over the Guadiana, he ordered a flying bridge to be thrown across, which was completed on the 15th of March, 1812. Over this Major-General Beresford passed, and immediately invested Badajos, with an army of fifteen thousand men. A covering army of thirty thousand occupied different positions near; and, including a division on its march from Beira, the whole of the allied forces now in Estremadura numbered fifty-one thousand.

The garrison of the enemy, composed of French, Hessian and Spanish troops, was five thousand strong. Phillipon, its brave commander, had been busily occupied, since the last siege, in strengthening the defences of the place, and in procuring supplies for the expected invasion. Every family was obliged to keep three months' provision on hand, or leave the place, and every preparation was made for an obstinate and long continued resistance.

General Picton took the chief command of the assailants. He was alternately assisted by Generals Kempt, Colville, and Bowis.

The night of the 17th was ushered in by a violent storm of wind and rain. It was extremely dark and uncomfortable; but, as the loud roar of the tempest would effectually drown the noise of the pick-axes, eighteen hundred men were ordered to break ground only one hundred and sixty yards from the Picurina. They were accompanied by a guard of two thousand men. So rapidly did they work, that, though it was late when they commenced, before morning they had completed a communication four thousand feet in length, and a parallel six hundred yards long, three feet deep, and three wide. The next night these works were enlarged, and two batteries traced out. To destroy these works was now the first object of the besieged.

On the 19th, thirteen hundred of their number stole out of the city, unobserved, into the communication, and began to destroy the parallel. They were soon discovered, however, and driven away. As they rode up, part of the French cavalry entered into a mock contest, giving the countersign in Portuguese, and were thus permitted to pass the pickets; but they soon betrayed their real character, and our troops, hastily seizing their arms, drove them back to the castle, with a loss of three hundred men. One hundred and fifty of the British fell, and, unfortunately, Colonel Fletcher, the chief engineer, was badly wounded.

Owing to this circumstance, and the continued wet and

boisterous state of the weather, the works advanced slowly; but the batteries were at length completed. Owing to the heavy rains, the parallel remained full of water, and it was found impossible to drain it. But this was in some degree remedied by making an artificial bottom of sandbags.

One place yet remained, on the right bank of the Guadiana, which Wellington had not invested. The eagle eye of Phillipon soon perceived his advantage. He erected here three batteries, which completely swept our works with a most destructive fire; and its effect would have been yet greater, had it not been that the mud obstructed the bound of the bullets.

A courier was instantly despatched to the fifth division, stationed at Campo Mayor, for assistance. But misfortunes seldom come alone. The heavy rains had caused such a rise in the river, that the flying bridges were swept away, and the trenches filled with water. The provisions and ammunition of the army were still on the other side of the river, so that we were soon in want of both. To add to this, the earth thrown up for intrenchments became so saturated with water that it crumbled away, and our labours were for the time wholly suspended. A few days of fine weather, however, relieved us from our unpleasant situation. The river subsided, another flying bridge was constructed and row-boats obtained, so that the communication might not again be interrupted, under any circumstances.

On the 25th the reinforcement from Campo Mayor arrived, and the right bank of the Guadiana was immediately invested. The same day, our batteries were opened upon the fort. The enemy were by no means silent spectators of this invasion. They returned our fire with such vigour, that several of our guns were dismounted, and quite a number of officers killed. Marksmen were also stationed on the trenches, to shoot every one who should show his head over the parapet.

General Picton now resolved to take the fort by assault. Its external appearance did not indicate much strength, and he hoped for an easy victory.

But the event proved that these appearances were deceptive. The fort was strong; the ditch fourteen feet perpendicular, and guarded with thick, slanting poles, and from the top there were sixteen feet of an earthen slope. Seven guns were mounted on the walls, and two hundred men, each armed with two loaded muskets, stood ready to repel all intruders. Loaded shells were also ranged along the walls, to be pushed over, in case of an attack. General Kempt took the direction of the assault, which was arranged for the night of the 25th. Five hundred men were selected from the third division, of which two hundred were stationed in the communication of San Roque, to prevent any assistance reaching the fort from the town; one hundred occupied a position at the right of the fort, one hundred at the left, and the remainder were held as a reserve, under the command of Captain Powis.

About nine o'clock, the signal was given, and the troops moved forward. The night was very clear, although there was no moon; and the fort, which had loomed up in the darkness still and silent, as though untenanted, answered back the first shot of the assailants with a discharge that caused it to resemble a sheet of fire. The first attack was directed against the palisades in the rear; but the strength of these, and the destructive fire poured down upon them, obliged them to seek some weaker part.

They turned to the face of the fort; but here, the depth of the ditch, and the slanting stakes at the top of it, again baffled their attempts. The enemy lost not a moment in pouring their fire upon the assailants, and the loud death-screams told that the crisis was becoming more and more imminent. The alarm-bells in the city itself now rung out their shrill sounds, the guns on the walls and on the castle opened on the assailants, rockets were thrown up by the besieged, and the answering shots from the trenches served to increase the tumult. All eyes were turned in the direction of the fort.

A battalion, hastily sent out from the city, advanced to its aid; but they had scarcely entered the communication, when the troops stationed there rushed to the onset, and in a few moments they were driven back within the walls. By the light of those streams of fire, which ascended every moment from the Picurina, dark forms might be seen struggling on the ramparts, in all the energy of determined contest. Continued rounds of artillery had broken down the palisades in front, and the assailants were fighting, hand to hand, for an entrance.

The party in the rear of the fort had thrown their ladders, like bridges, across the ditch, resting them on the slanting stakes, and springing on them, drove back their guards. Fifty men, bearing axes, now discovered the gate, which soon fell beneath their blows, and they rushed in to a nearer contest. The little garrison, stern in their resistance, did what they could. Powis, Gips, Holloway and Oates, fell on the ramparts. Nixon, Shaw, and Rudd, were not long behind. Scarcely an officer was left; and yet the struggle continued.

At length, when only eighty-six men remained, they surrendered, and the Picurina passed to the allies. Only one hour had that fierce conflict lasted, yet of our troops four officers and fifty men had fallen, and fifteen officers and two hundred and fifty men were wounded. Phillipon felt deeply the loss of this fort. He did not conceal from his soldiers the increase of danger to their city from it; but he stimulated their courage by reminding them that death was far preferable to an abode in the English prison-ships. They deeply felt that appeal, and, with the first dawn of light, their guns were manned with renewed activity.

These were turned against the fort, and so raked it that it was impossible for our troops to remain there, and it was deserted. This victory gave fresh courage to the besiegers. Our whole force was occupied, the three succeeding nights, in erecting new batteries, and in extending the parallels and communications. In the daytime, comparatively little could be done, as the fire from the town so galled the workmen. Repeatedly they dismounted our guns, and destroyed the defences which had been erected to shield the labourers, so that we were obliged to wait until the darkness prevented their marksmen from taking aim, in order to carry on our works.

The night of the 27th, an attempt was made to destroy the dam, which had been built for the purpose of forming an inundation, and lessening the space where our troops could work; but the moon had now made her appearance, and shone so brightly that the effort was unsuccessful.

On this night a most daring feat was performed by one of the French. Having disguised himself, he crept over the wall, and concealed himself until he had caught the watchword for the night. Then, boldly mingling with the troops, he proceeded to the works. Here the engineer had placed a line to mark the direction of the sap. Just before the workmen arrived, he moved the string, until he brought it within complete range of the castle guns. The men commenced work at once, but the light of the moon enabled the guns to tell with fearful precision upon them; and it was not until a severe loss had been sustained, that the mistake was discovered. Meanwhile, the intruder stole quietly back to his old quarters, which he reached unmolested.

Soult, trusting to the strong intrenchments of the place, had but little fear that it would finally surrender; but he knew a hard-fought battle was inevitable. He therefore endeavoured, as much as possible, to concentrate his forces near;

but, while they were marching for this purpose, Graham and Hill attacked their flanks, and forced them to take another direction. The whole of the Spanish army now moved on to the Ronda hills, and threatened to attack Seville. This movement obliged Soult to detach a large part of his army to the assistance of this city, and had, as the event proved, fatally delayed his march to Badajos.

On the 30th, Wellington received information that Soult had resumed his march, and would soon arrive; but this news only served to hasten the preparations for the attack. Forty-eight pieces of artillery were now constantly playing against the San Roque, and the siege advanced at all points. Still the San Roque stood firm. General Picton was the more anxious for its destruction, as the inundation, which was caused by the dam, and protected by this lunette, prevented the free action of the troops.

On the night of the 1st of April, several brave fellows determined to see if they could not accomplish by *stratagem* what open force had failed to effect. Two officers placed themselves at the head of a small company of sappers. Under cover of the darkness, and their motions encumbered by the powder they were obliged to carry, they stole rapidly, but noiselessly, into the camp of the enemy. It was, indeed, a dangerous experiment. The least noise, the slightest accident, might alarm the sentinel; and then, they well knew, none would return to tell their fate. Scarcely venturing to breathe, they reached, in safety, a spot near the place. One of the officers then went to examine the dam. During his absence, the rest of the party could see the sentinel, as he approached within a very few feet of where they lay concealed. They saw, if they could dispose of him without noise, they might probably accomplish their aim undiscovered. The officer, having examined the dam, now returned, just as the sentinel approached.

"Now, boys, is your time," he whispered. "Remember, one word, one sound, and we are lost." Riquet, a powerful Irishman, selected for this purpose, seized his cloak, and stood prepared. As the man was passing, he sprang forward, and, throwing his cloak over him, he was in an instant gagged and bound. Then, rapidly and silently, the powder was placed against the dam, the train laid, and the match applied. They waited a moment, to see that it was not extinguished, and then hastily retreated.

A few moments passed, and the loud explosion was the first intelligence the enemy had of the intrusion. All eyes were bent anxiously upon the spot, but our hopes were destined to a sad disappointment. The dam stood firm, and the inundations still remained. But, although this brave attempt had failed, it soon became apparent to our general that the crisis was rapidly approaching. The bastions of the Trinidad and the Santa Maria had already given way; the breaches were daily enlarging, and hope grew strong that we should succeed in reducing the place before Soult should arrive. Nor were the enemy blind to their danger. They had already built a strong intrenchment behind the walls. Now they converted the nearest houses and garden-walls into a third line of defence.

CHAPTER 9

I Take Part in the Assault

Rumours were continually circulating that the French army was close at hand; but they were so uncertain that no dependence could be placed upon them. About this time, however, certain intelligence was brought that Soult had effected a junction with Drouet and Daricoa, and was already at Albuera. No time was then to be lost. Wellington himself examined the breaches, and pronounced them practicable, and the night of the 6th of April was fixed for the assault. Rapidly the news circulated among the army, and eighteen thousand daring soldiers burned for that attack, that was to carry to posterity so dreadful a tale.

I shall never forget the effect on our own regiment, when it was announced. General Sponsbury himself bore the tidings, and asked if our regiment—the 28th of foot—was willing to lead the assault upon the castle. This offer had already been made to the colonels of the 10th and 17th regiments; but their men were suffering so severely from a disease in the eyes, called the *Jamaica Sands*, that they declined the honour. "My men have their eyes open, at such a time, general," answered our brave colonel; "nor is their leader ever blind to the interests of king and country." Then, turning to us, he cried, "What say you, my lads? Are you willing to take the front ranks in this attack?" A loud shout gave its affirmative to this appeal. Every heart thrilled at the honour thus conferred, although all knew how perilous such a distinction must necessarily be.

The dreaded yet longed-for night drew on, and our officers were busily engaged in arranging the order of the attack, and in preparing the men for their duty. Picton's division was to cross the Rivillas river, and scale the castle walls, which were from eighteen to twenty feet in height, furnished with every means of destruction, and so narrow at the top that their defenders could easily reach and overturn the ladders.

To Leith was appointed the distant bastion of San Vincente, where the glacis was mined, the ditch deep, the scarp thirty feet high, and the defenders of the parapet armed with three loaded muskets each, that their first fire should be as deadly as possible.

The 4th and light divisions were to march against the breaches, well furnished with ladders and axes, preceded by storming parties of five hundred men, with their forlorn hopes. Major Wilson, of the 48th, was directed to storm San Roque, and to General Power was assigned the bridge head.

The morning had been very clear, but, as night approached, clouds covered the horizon, as if to veil the bloody scenes of the night. Fog rose thick from the rivers over every object, thus rendering the darkness more complete. Unusual stillness prevailed, although low murmurs pervaded the trenches, and, on the ramparts, lights occasionally flitted here and there. Every few moments the deep-toned voices of the sentinels broke in upon our ears, proclaiming that "all was well in Badajos."

The possession of this place had become a point of honour with the soldiers on both sides. Three times had the French seen their foes sit down before these almost impregnable walls. Twice had they been obliged to retire, with heavy losses. The memory of these disasters, revenge for those who had fallen, hatred of their foes, and a strong desire for glory, now nerved each British arm for the contest; while the honour of the French nation, the approval of their idolized emperor, and, more than all, the danger to which their families would be exposed in case of failure, combined with an equal thirst for glory, awakened all the ardent enthusiasm of the French.

At ten o'clock a simultaneous assault was to be made on the castle, the San Roque, the breaches, the Pardaleras, San Vincente, and the bridge head, on the other side of the Guadiana.

The enemy were, as yet, all unconscious of the design of our general, and the dark array of the British moved slowly and silently forward. Every heart was full; for, although now unusual quiet reigned, every one knew that it was but the prelude to that hour when death, in its most terrible and ghastly forms, would be dealt on every side. In one short half-hour the signal was to be given,—nay, even that little time was lost. A lighted carcass was thrown up from the castle, and fell at the very feet of the men in the third division, casting a lurid and glaring light for yards around. The wild shout of alarm, the hurried tones of the signal-bells, and the tumultuous rushing of the soldiers, proclaimed that our array was discovered. Not a moment was to be lost. "Forward, my men, forward!" passed from rank to rank. One wild, long, deafening shout, responded, and then the besiegers dashed onward. In a moment a circle of fire seemed to surround the doomed city.

Our own division, under charge of General Kempt, had crossed the narrow plank that constituted the bridge over the Rivillas, under a heavy fire of musketry, and then, re-forming, ran hastily up the rugged hill, to the foot of the castle. Scarcely had we reached the walls, when our brave general fell, severely wounded. His faithful aids-de-camp carried him from the field; and, as they were passing to the trenches, he met General Picton,—who, hurt by a fall, and unprepared for the advance of the signal, had been left in the camp,—hastening onward. A few hurried words passed between them, and General Picton ran on, to find his brave soldiers already ascending the heavy ladders they had placed against the castle walls. And well might those men be called brave, who dared attempt to ascend those ladders, in spite of the showers of heavy stones, logs of wood, and bursting shells, that rolled off the parapet,—regardless, too, of that ceaseless roll of musketry, that was telling with such fearful precision on their flanks,—forgetting, apparently, that, even should they live to reach the, top, they could scarcely hope to survive the shock of that formidable front of pikes and bayonets that rose to meet them.

Deafening shouts echoed on every side, as the besieged endeavoured to throw down those heavy ladders; and these were answered back by the groans of the dying, and the shrieks of the soldiers that were crushed by their fall. Yet, not for a moment daunted, those behind sprang on to the remaining ladders, and strove which first should meet the death that seemed inevitable. But their courage was fruitless. Every ladder was thrown down, and loud shouts of victory ran along the walls. But the British, though foiled, were not subdued.

They fell back a few paces, and re-formed. Colonel Ridge then sprang forward, and, seizing a ladder, placed it against the lowest part of the castle wall, loudly calling to his men to follow. Officer Canch succeeded in placing another beside him, and in an instant they were fighting upon the ramparts. Ridge fell, pierced with a hundred wounds; but, ere his assailants had time to strike again, those ladders had poured their living load into the castle, and, step by step, were its brave defenders forced, fighting, into the street. Here a reinforcement induced them to pause, and a hard-fought conflict ensued. But their assistants came too late,—the castle was ours.

While these events were passing at the castle, more terrific, more maddening, if possible, was the contest at the breaches. Just as the firing at the castle commenced, two divisions reached the glacis. The flash of a single musket from the covered way was the signal that the French were ready, and yet all was still and dark. Hay packs were thrown hastily into the ditches, and five hundred men sprang down the ladders, which were placed there, without any opposition. "Why was this ominous stillness? But the assailants had hardly time to ask, when a bright light shot up from the darkness, and revealed all the horrors of the scene.

The ramparts were crowded with dark figures and glittering arms, while, below, the red columns of the British were rushing on, like streams of burning lava. A crash of thunder followed that bright light, and hundreds of shells and powder-barrels dashed the ill-fated stormers into a thousand atoms. One instant the light division paused, and then, as if maddened by that terrific sight, they flew down the ladders, or leaped into the gulf below. A blaze of musketry poured its dazzling light into the ditch, as the fourth division came up, and descended with equal fury. But the enemy had made, at the bottom of the ditch, a deep cut, which was filled with water. Into this snare the head of the division fell, and more than a hundred men were drowned. Those behind checked not an instant, but, turning to the left, came to an unfinished intrenchment, which they mistook for the breaches. It was covered in a moment; but, beyond it, still lay a deep and wide chasm, between them and the ramparts they wished to gain. Confusion necessarily ensued, for the assailants still crowded on, until the ditch was full, and even then the press continued.

Not for one moment ceased the roar of the musketry upon those crowded troops, and the loud shouts of the enemy, mingled with the din of bursting grenades and shells.

The roaring guns were answered back by the iron howitzers from the battery, while the horrid explosions of the powder-barrels, the whizzing flight of the blazing splinters, and the loud commands of the officers, increased the confusion. Through all this the great breach was at length reached, and the British trusted that the worst was over; but, deep in those ruins, ponderous beams were set, and, firmly fixed on their top, glittered a terrible array of sword-blades, sharp-pointed and keen-edged, while ten feet before even that could be reached, the ascent was covered with loose planks, studded with sharp iron points, which penetrated the feet of the foremost, and sent them rolling back on the troops behind.

Behind these sword-points, the shouting Frenchmen stood rejoicing in their agony, and poured in their fire with ceaseless rapidity; for every man had a number of muskets, and each one of these, beside the ordinary charge, was loaded with a cylinder of wood, full of leaden slugs, which scattered like hail, when discharged. Hundreds of men had fallen, and hundreds more were dropping; but still the heroic officers rushed on, and called for new trials. Yet, there glittered the sword-blades, firm, immovable; and who might penetrate such a barrier? Yet, so zealous were the men themselves, that those behind strove to push the forward ranks on to the blades, that they might thus themselves ascend on a bridge made of their bodies; but they frustrated this attempt of dropping down, for none could tell who fell from choice, and who by the effect of that dreadful fire, and many who fell unhurt never rose again, crushed by the crowd.

For a little while after the commencement of this terrible attack, military order was preserved; but the tumult and noise was such, that no command could be distinctly heard; and the constant falling and struggling of the wounded, who sought to avoid being trampled upon, broke the formations, and order was impossible. Yet, officers of all stations would rush out, and, followed by their men, make a desperate assault on that glittering steel, and only fall back to swell the pile of dead and dying. Two hours were spent in these vain efforts, and then the remaining soldiers turned sadly and slowly away; for they felt that the breach of the Trinidad was, indeed, impregnable. An opening still remained in the curtain of the Santa Maria bastion, and to this they directed their steps; but they found the approach to it impeded by deep holes and cuts, and their fearfully lessening numbers told how useless the attempt would be.

Gathering in dark groups, they leaned despairingly on their muskets, and looked with sullen desperation at the ramparts of the Trinidad, where the enemy were seen, by the light of the fire-balls which they threw up, aiming their guns with fearful precision, and tauntingly asking, "Why they did not come into Badajos? " And now, unwilling to be finally conquered, Captains Nicholas and Shaw, with fifty men, collected from all regiments, made one more desperate attempt to reach the Santa Maria breach. Already had they passed the deep cuts, and toiled over two-thirds of the dangerous ground, when a discharge of musketry levelled every man, except Shaw, to the earth. Nicholas, and a large proportion of the rest, were mortally wounded.

After this, no further attempt was made; and yet the soldiers would not retire, but remained passive and unflinching, under the fire of the enemy. It was now midnight. Already two thousand brave men had fallen, when Wellington, who was watching the progress of the attack from a height close to the quarries, sent orders that the troops should retire and re-form for a second assault. But so great was the confusion, that many of the officers did not receive the orders, and so endeavoured to prevent the soldiers from leaving, which occasioned many deaths.

But the gallant defenders of Badajos, although successful at the breaches, found that there was no time to look idly on. The whole city was girdled by fire. The third division still maintained its ground at the castle; the fifth were engaged at the Pardaleres, and on the right of the Guadiana, while General Walker's brigade was escalading the bastion of San Vincente. This brigade had stolen silently along the banks of the river, the noise of its ripple having drowned the sound of their foot-steps until they reached the barrier gate. Just then the explosion took place at the breaches; and by its light the French sentinels discovered their assailants. In an instant, a sharp musketry was opened upon them.

The Portuguese troops, panic-struck, threw down the scaling-ladders which had been intrusted to them; but the British snatched them up, and reared them against the walls, which, in this place, were thirty feet high. Unfortunately, the ladders were too short, and this placed them in a most perilous and uncomfortable position. A small mine was sprung beneath their feet, adding its quota to the fearful number of the dead; beams of wood and shells, fraught with living fire, were rolled upon their heads, while showers of grape from the flanks swept the ditch, dealing death-blows thick and fast on every side. But, fortunately for our troops, the reinforcement to assist in the defence of the castle was just at this time called for, and a part of the walls lower than the rest was left unmanned.

Three ladders were hastily placed here, but they were still too short. But British valour and ingenuity soon overcame this difficulty. A soldier, raised in the arms of his comrades, sprang to the top; another followed. These drew their comrades after them, and soon, in spite of the constant fire which the French kept up, they ascended in such numbers, that they could not be driven back. Dividing, on their entrance, one-half entered the town, while the other, following the ramparts, attacked and won three bastions.

Just as the last was yielding, General Walker fell, covered with wounds. A soldier, who stood near him, cried out, "A mine! A mine!" At that word, those troops which had crossed the strong barrier, whom neither the deepness of the ditch nor the height of the wall could appal, who flinched not a moment at the deadly fire of the enemy, shrank back at a chimera of their own raising. Their opponents saw their advantage, and, making a firm and deadly charge, drove them from the ramparts. But, before the French had time to rejoice in their victory, a reserve, under Colonel Nugent, made its appearance, and the fleeing soldiers returned, and soon gained the field.

The party who had entered the town at the first attack on San Vincente pursued their way through the streets. They met with no opposition, however. All was still and silent as the grave, and yet the streets were flooded with light, and every house illuminated. Sounding their bugles, they advanced to the great square of the town, but still met no enemy. All was bright and still, except that low murmurs were heard from behind the lattices, and occasionally a shot was fired at them from under the doors. Hence, leaving the square, they repaired to the breaches, and attempted to surprise the garrison, by attacking them in their rear. But they found them on the alert, and were soon obliged to return to the streets. But the English were now pouring in on every side, and the brave defenders of the ramparts and the breaches turned to defend their homes. A short and desultory fight followed. Generals Viellande and Phillipon, brave and determined to the last, were both wounded; and, gradually falling back, they retreated, with a few hundred soldiers, to San Christoval, where they surrendered to Lord Fitzroy Somerset. Then loud shouts of "Victory! Victory!" resounded through the streets, and found its joyful echo in many hearts.

Chapter 10

After the Fall of Badajoz

During this siege, five thousand men and officers had fallen; thirty-five hundred having lost their lives the night of the assault,—twenty-four hundred at the breaches alone. If any one would picture to himself the terrible scenes that occurred at this spot, let him imagine a lot of less than a hundred square yards, which, in the short space of little more than two hours, was deluged by the blood of twenty-four hundred men. Nor did all these fall by sudden death. Some perished by steel, some by shot, some were drowned, some crushed and mangled by heavy weights, others trampled down by the crowd, and hundreds dashed to pieces by the fiery explosions; and all this occurred where the only light was the intense glare of the explosions, and the lurid flame of the burning dead, which came to mingle its horrible stench with the sickening odours of the gunpowder, and the nauseous smells of the exploding shells.

Here, too, the groans of the wounded were echoed back by the shrieks of the dying; and, ever and anon, between the roar of the artillery and the thunder of the bursting shells, were heard the bitter taunts of the enemy. Let any one imagine all this, I say, and they may have some faint ideas of the horrors of war. Yet, dreadful as this is, could the veil but drop here, the soldier's heart might still throb with pride, as he recounted the hard-fought battle, where valour stood pre-eminent, and none yielded, but to death, until the victory was won.

But there is still another dark and revolting page, which, in a history like this, designed to paint the horrors as well as the glories of war, it were not well to omit. I refer to the scenes which followed the victory, when Badajos lay at the mercy of its conquering foe. If there is one feature of war more repulsive than another, one from which every good feeling of the heart shrinks back appalled, it is from the scene which invariably follows, when permission is given to sack and plunder a conquered city. All restraint is laid aside. Men's passions, wound up almost to frenzy by the exciting and maddening scenes through which they have passed, will have a vent; and no sorrow is too holy, no place too sacred, to shield its occupant from the storm. Our men scattered themselves through the city, all with liberty to do what they pleased, to take what they wanted.

Houses were broken open, and robbed. If any resistance was made, death was the certain penalty; and often death in such a form that a soldier's fate would have been mercy. All, it is true, were not alike. In such an army there are always brave men, who, even in such an hour, would scorn to commit a dishonourable action, and these seconded the attempts of our officers to preserve at least a semblance of order; but they were too few to accomplish much. All the dreadful passions of human nature were excited, and they would have way. Many lost their lives in vain attempts to check the cruelty and lust and drunkenness of their own soldiers. For two days and nights Badajos resounded with the shrieks and piteous lamentations of her defenceless victims, with groans and shouts and imprecations, varied by the hissing of fires from houses first plundered, then destroyed, the crashing of doors and windows, and the almost ceaseless report of muskets used in violence. It was not until the third day that the soldiers, exhausted by their own excesses, could be collected in sufficient numbers to bury the dead of their own regiments, while many of the wounded perished solely from want of necessary care.

I had imagined that the miseries of intemperance were no unfamiliar sight to me; yet never before, or since, has it been my lot to meet the madness which characterized the eager search for liquor, on every side. An instance that occurred in our own regiment, I will relate. Several of our men, and among them some that I had known in Ireland, and should never have suspected of such conduct, broke into a cellar where was stored a large quantity of wine. There were many casks, and some of them contained wine that bore the brand of scores of years.

They tore down the doors for tables, and commenced their mad feast. Bottles half emptied were thrown across the cellar, and what would have sufficed a regiment for months, was recklessly poured upon the floor. Unconscious, or not caring what they did, they stopped not to draw the wine, but, knocking in the head of the casks, proceeded to try their various qualities. At length, overcome by intoxication, they sank upon the floor, and paid the penalty of their rashness with their lives; for, when a diligent search was made for absentees, they were discovered actually drowned in the wine. Many were burned to death in houses which they themselves had fired.

For my own part, I had been fortunate enough to pass through all the horrors of the siege, and the bloody scenes of the assault, unhurt. Excitement had rendered me reckless of danger, and I hurried on, scarce knowing where I was or what I did. Now that this had passed, I felt exhausted and weary, and very thirsty. My comrade and myself resolved that our first search should be for something to drink. We hurried on, until we reached a large store, where we thought we should find some liquor. The fastenings of the outer door soon yielded to our efforts, but the door to the cellar we found it impossible to open or break down. Just at this moment, a band of pioneers happened to be passing, who always carry with them huge hatchets.

We called to them, and, with their assistance, soon made our way to the cellar. But here a great disappointment awaited us. We found no liquor, but only two tiers of firkins, used for holding butter. One of our men, in anger, struck his hatchet into one of them, when, to our great surprise, out rolled whole handfuls of doubloons. We then struck the heads of the firkins with the butt-ends of our muskets, but could not break them. The hatchets, however, soon completed the work. When the heads were knocked out, the money was so firmly pressed together that it came out in one solid mass. Each one of us then took what we pleased.

I placed three handfuls in my comrade's knapsack, and he did the same by me. I then filled my haversack, and even my stockings, with the precious treasure. Part of our company remained as guard, while the rest went to report to our commander the discovery we had made. I soon found that I had stored more money than I was able to carry, so I threw a part of it in an old well. Our commander immediately sent a detachment of men to empty the cellar, and they brought away no less than eight mules' burden of gold. I cannot now recall its exact amount, but such was its value that our officers determined to send it to Brussels, when the army should leave Badajos.

We take the following description of the scenes to which we have above referred from an eye-witness. He says:

It has been the practice of modern historians to describe, in the glowing language of exaggerated eulogy, every act done by the British and their allies, while their pens have been equally busy in vilifying and defaming all who were opposed to them. Perhaps there is no circumstance to which this applies with more force than the description usually given of the conduct of the British armies and their allies after the taking of Badajos. While their gallantry is praised to the utmost, their evil deeds are left to find the light as they may; but 'foul deeds will rise, though all the earth overwhelm them.'

Before six o'clock on the morning of the 7th of April, all organization among the assaulting columns had ceased, and a scene of plunder and cruelty that it would be difficult to find a parallel for took place. The army, so orderly the preceding day,—so effective in its organizations,—seemed all at once transformed into a vast band of brigands. The horde of Spaniards, as well as Portuguese women and men, that now eagerly sought for admission to plunder, augmented the number of this band to what the army had been before the battle; and twenty thousand persons, armed with all power to act as they thought fit, and almost all armed with weapons which could be used at the pleasure of the bearers, for the purpose of enforcing any wish they might seek to gratify, were let loose upon this devoted city. Subject to no power of control from others, intoxication caused them to lose all restraint on themselves.

If the reader can for a moment fancy a fine city, containing an immense population, among which may be reckoned a proportion of the finest women Spain, or perhaps the world, can boast of,—if he could fancy that population and these women left to the mercy of twenty thousand infuriated and licentious soldiers, for two days and two nights, he can well imagine the horrors enacted in Badajos. Wine and spirit stores were first forced open, and casks of the choicest wines and brandy dragged into the streets; and, when the men had drank as much as they fancied, the heads of the vessels were stove in, or the casks broken, so that the liquor ran about in streams. In the town were large numbers of animals,—sheep, oxen, and horses,—belonging to the garrison. These were among the first things taken possession of; and the wealthy occupier of many a house was glad to be allowed the employment of conducting them to our camp, as, by so doing, he got away from a place where his life was not worth a minute's purchase.

Terrible as was this scene, it was not possible to avoid occasionally laughing; for the *conducteur* was generally not only compelled to drive a herd of cattle, but also obliged to carry the bales of plunder taken by his employer perhaps from his own house. And the stately gravity with which the Spaniard went through his work, dressed in short breeches, frilled shirt, and a hat and plumes, followed by our ragamuffin soldiers with fixed bayonets, presented a scene that Cruikshank himself would have been puzzled to delineate justly. The plunder so captured was deposited under a guard composed principally of soldiers' wives. A few hours were sufficient to despoil the shops of their property.

Night then closed in, and then a scene took place that pen would fail to describe. Insult and infamy, fiendish acts of violence and open-handed cruelty, everywhere prevailed. Age, as well as youth, was alike unrespected, and perhaps not one house, and scarcely a person, in this vast town, escaped injury. War is a terrible engine, and when once set in motion, it is not possible to calculate when or where it will stop.

The 8th of April was a fearful day for the inhabitants.

The soldiers had become so reckless that no person's life, of whatever sex, rank, or station, was safe. If they entered a house that had not been despoiled of its furniture and wines, they were at once destroyed. If it was empty, they fired at the windows, or at the inmates, or often at each other. Then they would sally into the streets, and amuse themselves by firing at the church bells in the steeples, or at any one who might be passing. Many of the soldiers were killed, while carrying away their plunder, by the hands of those who, a few hours before, would have risked their own lives to protect them. Hundreds of these fellows took possession of the best warehouses, and acted as merchants; these were ejected by a stronger party, who, after a fearful strife, would displace them, only themselves to give place to others, with terrible loss of life.

To put a stop to such a frightful scene, it was necessary to use some forbearance, as well as severity; for, to have punished all who were guilty would have been to decimate the army. In the first instance, parties from those regiments that had least participated in. the combat were ordered into the town to collect the hordes of stragglers, that filled the streets with crimes too horrible to detail; and, when this measure was found inadequate, a brigade of troops were marched into the city, and were directed to stand by their arms, while any marauders remained. Gibbets and triangles were erected, and many of the men were flogged. A few hours so employed were sufficient to purge the town of the robbers that still lurked in the streets, many of whom were Spaniards and Portuguese, not connected with the army, and infinitely worse than our troops.

Towards evening tranquillity began to return; but it was a fearful quiet, and might be likened to a ship at sea, which, after having been plundered and dismasted by pirates, should be left floating on the ocean, without a morsel of food to supply the wants of its crew, or a stitch of canvas to cover its naked masts. By degrees, however, the inhabitants returned, and families left alive again became reunited; yet there was scarce a family that did not mourn its dead.

The same writer says:

Early on the morning of the 9th of April, a great concourse of Spaniards, from the neighbouring villages, thronged our lines. They came to purchase the booty captured by our men; and each succeeding hour increased the supply of their wants, numerous and varied as they were, and our camp had the appearance of a vast market. Some of the soldiers realized upwards of one thousand dollars from the sale, and almost all gained handsomely by an enterprise in which they had displayed so much devotion and bravery; and it is only to be lamented that they tarnished laurels so nobly won, by traits of barbarity which, for the sake of human nature, we hope have not often found a parallel.

It was not until order was in some measure restored that the wounded and dead could be attended to; but now graves were dug, and the mangled remains, so lately full of life and activity, burning with high hopes and fond anticipations, were laid away, adding their numbers to the vast pile of victims sacrificed to that Moloch—war. It is said that when Wellington learned the number of the fallen, and the extent of his loss in the death of those brave men, a passionate burst of tears told how much he was affected by it.

For a few days Wellington lingered near Badajos, hoping that Soult, to whom Phillipon had sent the fatal news even in the confusion of his surrender, would be tempted from his intrenchments to risk a battle with the allies, while the troops were flushed with victory. But this general, although feeling deeply the loss of one of his most impregnable fortresses, found himself too much occupied with the other division of the allied army to venture on such a course.

It was Wellington's intention, in case this battle did not take place, to proceed immediately to Andalusia; but, learning that the Spanish general had failed to garrison the fortresses already taken in a suitable manner, he was obliged to alter his own course of action, in order to secure former conquests. While he remained here, his time was busily occupied in repairing the breaches, in levelling the trenches, and restoring the injured fortifications. This being done, he placed here, as a garrison, two regiments of Portuguese, and marched himself, with the main body of his troops, upon Beira.

CHAPTER 11

The Adventures of Colquhoun Grant

Soon after our army left Badajos, the remarkable and interesting adventures of Sir Colquhoun Grant, who was an officer in our army, attracted general attention; and, though I did not myself learn all the particulars I am about to relate until after my return from the continent, they are in themselves of so interesting a nature, and so closely connected with the success of our arms in the Peninsula, that I trust my readers will deem these reasons a sufficient excuse for their introduction here.

Intelligence had been brought to our commander that the army of Portugal, under Marmont, was concentrating on the Tonnes, and that they were intending to attack the fortresses of Almeida and Ciudad.

If this was indeed so, it was all-important that he should immediately march to their relief, as their garrisons and stores were far too weak to sustain an attack or stand a siege. But, as Wellington could not believe that the French general would take what seemed to him so imprudent a course, he suspected that this information, was only a ruse to draw him from his position. It was absolutely necessary that he should know the truth. Among his troops was an officer named Colquhoun Grant. Gentlemanly and peculiarly attractive in his manners, bold even to the utmost daring, and yet with so much subtlety of genius, tempered with the wisest discre-

161

tion, he seemed exactly fitted by nature for the dangerous and delicate office which our commander-in-chief intrusted to him, which was to watch Marmont's proceedings, and, if possible, to learn his true intentions. He secured the services of a Spanish peasant, named Leon, whose own life it had been his good fortune to preserve in a skirmish, and whose only sister Grant had rescued from the guerrillas, just as they were bearing her off. So grateful was poor Leon, that he esteemed himself only too happy in being allowed to share his master's danger in this perilous enterprise.

Having passed the Tormes in the night, as morning was breaking, he rode boldly up to the French camp, dressed in his own uniform and followed by his servant. In answer to the challenge of the sentinel on duty, he informed him that he was the bearer of a message to one of the principal officers of the French army, and was admitted without hesitation.

The wife of this officer had accompanied her husband to Spain, and was in Badajos at the time of its surrender. During the excesses which followed, her house was entered by some ruffians, and she would have fallen a victim to their rage, had it not been for the timely interference of Grant, who rescued her from her assailants, and bore her to a place of comparative safety. As a small memento of her gratitude, when the army left, she wrote him a note expressing her heartfelt thanks, and accompanied it by a valuable ring. Armed with the note and ring, he proceeded at once to the tent of the officer, who gladly received him as the bearer of information from his wife, and invited him to share the hospitalities of the camp.

Here he remained for three days, and, by his adroitness in conversation, obtained exact information as to Marmont's object, and the preparation he had made, both of provisions and scaling-ladders. While there, each day a Spanish peasant made his appearance in the camp, laden with fruit for sale; and while Grant was apparently busy in purchasing, he conveyed to him notes of his information, which were immediately carried to Wellington.

Just before the night sentinels had taken their posts on the third evening, while he was in earnest conversation with a number of the French officers, he heard the low signal of the peasant outside the tent. He succeeded in excusing his absence in such a manner as not to attract observation, and received the alarming intelligence that he was known to be in the French cantonments, and that a general order was even now circulating, giving a description of his person, and commanding the soldiers to use their utmost exertions to secure him. Guards had already been stationed in a circle round the army, and escape seemed impossible. Not a moment was to be lost. Leaving his horse with Leon, who was to meet him at Huerta at daybreak, he crept past the sleeping soldiers, and succeeded in reaching that village undiscovered. But it was now daybreak, and the outward circle of the guards was yet to be passed. Before him lay a deep river, fordable only at one point, and along which videttes were posted, constantly patrolling back and forward, meeting at the ford, while the whole battalion was engaged in the search. Yet these difficulties did not daunt him.

Leon and Grant met at the house of a peasant, one of his agents, who had several of his friends, wrapped in their large Spanish cloaks, ready to assist him. They advanced towards the ford, one of them leading his horse, and the others spreading their cloaks, as if estimating their comparative width. Under this cover, he stole along down to the ford. Here, waiting until the sentinels had separated their utmost distance, which was three hundred yards, he boldly mounted his horse, and dashed into the river. They both fired, but without success, and, without stopping to reload, pursued him. A wood lay directly before him. This covert he reached in safety, and was soon hid in its recesses. Here his faithful Leon joined him, and all pursuit of both was baffled. Grant here ascertained that the French were preparing to storm Ciudad Rodrigo, or, at least, that they conversed freely of doing so. From this fact, he judged it might be only a mask of their real intentions.

These, if possible, together with their numbers and the direction of their march, he wished to discover. He therefore concealed himself in the branches of a high tree, just where the road directs its course to the passes, and beneath which the whole army must proceed. Here he counted every battalion and gun, and found that their course was directed against Ciudad. When the last soldier was out of sight, he descended from the tree, and, entering the village they had just left, he discovered all the scaling-ladders securely stored. He immediately wrote to Wellington that he need have no fears for that fortress.

His next object was to discover whether Marmont was marching upon Castello Branco or Coimbra. To reach the former place, it was necessary to descend to the pass by a succession of ridges. He stationed himself on one of the lowest of these, thinking that the dwarf oaks, of which there was here a thick growth, would hide him; but, as the French officers were descending from the ridge above, they happened to spy him with their glasses, and despatched some dragoons in pursuit. Leon's lynx eyes, always on the watch, soon perceived them, and, alarming his master, they rode forward a short distance, and then wheeled in another direction. But now the alarm had spread, and all over the wood the soldiers were engaged in eager search.

Finding every pass beset by their enemies, they left their horses, and fled on foot through the thickest of the oaks. But these were not thick enough to veil them from the officers, on the higher ridges, who, by the waving of their hats, directed the chase. Efforts like these could not last long. Leon fell, exhausted, and Grant refused to yield to his entreaties to leave him.

The enemy soon made their appearance, and, in despite of the earnest entreaties and prayers of Grant, they killed poor Leon, and carried Grant to Marmont's tent. This general received him apparently with much kindness, and invited him to dinner. While seated at the table, he conversed freely with his prisoner, but closed by exacting from him a parole that he would not suffer himself to be released by the Partidas while passing through Spain. When Wellington discovered the capture of this faithful servant, he offered a reward of two thousand dollars to any one who would release him. Marmont then placed his prisoner under a strong escort, and sent him to France. He also sent with him a letter to the governor of Bayonne, designating him as a dangerous spy, and recommending the governor to send him, in irons, immediately to Paris.

The gentlemanly conduct of Grant, during his journey, and his lion-hearted bravery, so won upon the esteem of one of the officers of his escort, that he acquainted him with the contents of the letter, before reaching Bayonne. It was the custom for the prisoners, on their arrival in this city, to wait on the authorities, and procure a passport to Verdun. His friend the officer succeeded in delaying the delivery of Marmont's letter until these formalities had been attended to. Grant's object then would be to rejoin his regiment in Spain; but he well knew that the search for him would be made in that direction.

He, therefore, resolved to go to Paris, because he judged that if the governor of Bayonne did not succeed in recapturing him, he would, for his own security, suppress the letter, in hopes the matter would be no further thought of.

He therefore went directly to the hotels, and, finding that General Souham was going there on his return from Spain he boldly introduced himself) and requested permission to join his party. Now, Souham had often heard of Grant, and was extremely pleased to make his acquaintance, and of course yielded a ready assent to his proposal. On their way, he conversed freely with him about his adventures, little thinking that he was aiding him in one of the most skilful of them all.

While passing through Orleans, he had the good fortune to meet an English agent, who gave him a recommendation to another secret agent in Paris, whose assistance would be of great use to him in effecting his final escape. When he arrived in Paris, he took his leave of Souham, and then went directly to the house of the Parisian agent. This gentleman received him with much kindness, and having ascertained that no inquiry had been set on foot about his escape, furnished him with a sum of money, and recommended to him to take rooms in a very public street, and to attend and be interested in the amusements of the city. He even appeared at the theatres, and frequented the coffee-houses, as his friend was connected with the police, and would give him seasonable warning, in case he should be suspected.

Several weeks passed away in this manner, when it so happened that an American—one of his fellow-lodgers who was just preparing to return home—was taken suddenly ill, and died. The evening before his death, as Grant was sitting by his side, his passport was brought to him, and laid upon a table near. It occurred to Grant, that, in case of his death, he might possess himself of this passport without injury to any one, which he accordingly did, and proceeded at once with it, unquestioned, to the mouth of the Loire. He was delighted to find here a ship just ready to sail for America. He went on board and engaged his passage, and was told that the ship would sail by noon. An hour had not elapsed, how-ever, when a despatch was received from Paris, informing the captain that important reasons existed why he should delay his journey.

The captain, annoyed by this interference with his views, mentioned it to his passengers; and Grant, seeing at once that he was in danger, threw himself upon the captain's mer-cy, by frankly explaining to him his real situation. This officer kindly entered at once into his plans, advising him to assume the character of a discontented sailor. Grant then dressed as a sailor, and, with forty dollars in money which the captain gave him for that purpose, went to the American consul, and deposited in his hands the money, as a pledge that he would prosecute the captain for ill treatment, when he should ar-rive in the States. In return for this, the consul furnished him with the certificate of a discharged sailor) which permitted him to pass from port to port, as if in search of a ship.

He wandered about thus for some days, when one day he saw a boatman sitting idly in his boat, apparently with noth-ing to do. He accosted him, and, thinking that he might be moulded to his purpose, he offered him ten Napoleons, if he would row him to a small island which appeared in the distance, where English ships often stopped to take in water. The boatman agreed to do so that night. The evening was fair, and the boat made rapid progress. Already the island rose upon their view in the distance, and beyond it loomed up the dark masts of the English vessel which was the harbour of safety and happiness to Grant.

Already he had deemed himself almost beyond the reach of danger, when suddenly he perceived that the course of his guide was altered. He demanded the reason of this, but no answer was returned. Drawing a knife from his pocket, he was about to enforce his demand, when suddenly two men sprang up from the bottom of the boat, where they had been concealed, and he saw that to struggle against his fate would be useless. Still, his courage did not desert him. He would yet be free. The dastardly boatman offered to proceed to the island, if more money was paid him; but Grant, when he had promised his ten Napoleons, had spent the last of his little stock, and the boatman, notwithstanding his breach of contract, demanded the whole. This demand, with great coolness and the utmost resolution, was refused by Grant. One Napoleon he should have, but no more. The boatman threatened to denounce him to the police; but Grant, always prepared, told him, if he did, that he would at once accuse him of aiding the escape of a prisoner of war, and would adduce the great price of his boat as the proof of his guilt. This menace was too powerful to be resisted, and Grant was allowed to depart unmolested.

In a few days Grant engaged a fisherman, who, with his son, pursued his calling on the coast, to carry him to the island. The bargain was this time faithfully performed; but fortune seemed everywhere against him. There was not a ship at the island, and it was far too small for him to venture to try concealment there. His next course was to exchange clothes with the fisherman's son, and take his place in the boat. Having spent some time in fishing, they gradually bore off to the south, where rumour said a large English ship-of-war was to be found.

In a few hours they obtained a glimpse of her, and were steering that way, when a shot from a coast battery brought them to a full stop, and a boat full of soldiers put off to board them. Hope again died away in the heart of the adventurous traveller, at that dreaded sight; but he would not yet despair. The boat drew near, and the fisherman, poor and needy, had now an opportunity of enriching *himself,* by denouncing his passenger. But the old man was true to his trust. He assured the soldiers that Grant was his son; and, convinced of this, they only warned him not to go out of the reach of the guns of the battery, because the English vessel was on the coast. But the fisherman, having given all the fish he had caught to the soldiers, told them if he did not, his poor family would starve,—that this was their only dependence,—and assured them that he was so well acquainted with the coast that he could always escape the enemy.

His prayers and presents prevailed, and he was desired to wait under the battery till night, and then depart; but, under pretence of arranging his escape from the English vessel, he made the soldiers point out her bearings so exactly, that when the darkness came, he lost not a moment in proceeding on board, and the intrepid Grant soon found himself once more in safety on her quarterdeck. The vessel soon sailed for England, and Grant was received in London with all the popularity which his arduous services demanded, and might now have obtained an honourable release from the toilsome service in which he had been engaged; but he was a true soldier at heart, and loved the toil and bustle of the camp, with all its hardships, far better than the ease and comfort of courts. He asked but one favour of his royal master, and this was to select a French officer, of equal rank, who should be sent back to his own country, that no doubt might remain of the propriety of his escape.

This he received permission to do; and he visited one of the prisons, where the French were detained, for the purpose of making his selection. Judge what must have been his astonishment, when the first person he saw was the old fisherman who had so befriended him in his trouble! The recognition was mutual; and the old man, whose heart longed for the old familiar haunts of his childhood, out of sight of which he had never been before, felt once more the dawn of hope in his bosom, as he saw that face, so full of benevolence and kindness, bent on him in pitying sorrow. His story was soon told. He and his son, venturing on the pass which Grant had given him in return for his kindness, had ventured out to sea in too near proximity to an English vessel. The captain, totally unmindful of their papers, had sunk their little boat, their only property, and brought them away to inhabit an English prison, while his poor family was starving at home.

The indignant Grant could scarcely listen to the conclusion of the tale. He immediately obtained their release, made them a present of a sum of money and a new boat, and saw them once more embarked for France, blessing the happy hour when they had shown such kindness to one so richly deserving of it. He then returned himself to the Peninsula, and, within four months from the time of his capture, he was again on the Tonnes, watching the army of Marmont, and only mourning that poor Leon was no longer alive to accompany him.

CHAPTER 12

We Fight Bandits

Hoping that my readers will be interested in this long digression, I will return at once to my own story.

Before the victorious army of the allies left Badajos, Wellington determined to send a convoy to Brussels with the treasure and spoils found in that place. The regiments selected to form this convoy were the 28th, the 80th, and 87th and 43rd. We were to leave Badajos, and pass through the northern part of Spain to Pampeluna, and through the romantic gorge of the Roncesvalles to St. Jean Pied de Port, in France, and from this place take the most direct course to Brussels.

The day before our army was to leave for Beira was the day selected for our march. Our farewell words were soon spoken, and we were on our way. No event of consequence had marked our course until we were near Pampeluna. On the left of this place, near Roncesvalles, is the beautiful valley of Bastan, one of the most fertile and delightful valleys in Spain, and abounding in every species of plenty. From Pampeluna to Zabieta, the road passes over a gentle ascent. From Zabieta this ascent increases, and becomes extremely rough and fatiguing near the village of Borquette. From this village it begins to ascend very lofty mountains, but which are extremely fertile and well wooded. Immediately after passing Borquette, the road ascends a mountain, and then descends the same, when it enters upon the memorable plain of Roncesvalles, where happened that memorable defeat of Charlemagne, which has furnished so copious a theme for poetry and romance. As there are few who have not heard of this celebrated pass, perhaps the legend connected with it may not be uninteresting to my readers.

Several Moorish chiefs, in the north-western part of Spain, had implored the protection of this celebrated emperor, and invited him to accept their vassalage. He at once assembled an army, crossed the Pyrenees, penetrated as far as Saragossa, and received the submission of all the neighbouring lords. News of threatened hostilities on the Rhenish frontiers caused him to hasten his march onward. Dividing his army into two bodies, he advanced, in person, at the head of the first division, leaving all the baggage with the rear guard, which comprised a strong force, and was commanded by some of the most renowned of his chieftains, among whom was Roland, the nephew of Charlemagne.

Mounted on heavy horses, and loaded with a complete armour of iron, the soldiers pursued their march through the narrow passes of the Pyrenees, without suspecting the neighbourhood of an enemy. The king himself, with his first division, passed from these intricate woods and narrow defiles unmolested; but when the rear body, following leisurely at a considerable distance, had reached this wild and lonely valley, the woods and rocks around them suddenly bristled into life, and they were attacked on all sides by the perfidious Gascons, whose light arms, swift arrows, and knowledge of the country; gave them every advantage over their opponents.

In the first panic and confusion, the Franks were driven down to the bottom of the pass, embarrassed by their arms and baggage. The Gascons pressed them on every point, and slaughtered them like a herd of deer, singling them out with their arrows from above, and rolling down the rocks upon their heads. Never wanting in courage, they fought until the last moment, and died unconquered. Roland and his companions, the twelve peers of France, after innumerable deeds of valour, were slain with the rest; and the Gascons, satiated with carnage, and rich in plunder, dispersed among the mountains, leaving Charlemagne to seek fruitlessly for vengeance.

During the lapse of many centuries, tradition has hung about this famous spot, and the memory of Roland and his companions has been consecrated in a thousand shapes throughout the country. When we entered this famous pass, we could but recall the legends connected with it. The mountains rose high and towering to the skies on either side. Far up their rocky sides we could see mountain paths descending, while here and there a shelf would exist that might give a standing-place to a body of men. Huge crags seemed to bid defiance even to the fleet steps of the mountain goat, while deep caverns opened their mouths on every side, giving shelter to the hordes of banditti which always infest those regions.

The stroke of Roland's sword upon the rocks was pointed out to us by our guides; while, just beneath, we noticed patches of the beautiful little wild-flower of the Pyrenees, which is called the casque of Roland. I know of no fitter place for the assault which took place here; certainly none which could give the assailants a better advantage. But, ominous as the scenery appeared, we crossed this famous pass in safety, and emerged, with gladdened and lightened hearts, on the plain beyond, where rises the beautiful and venerable abbey of Roncesvalles, whose moss-clad walls, which have felt so heavily, and yet sustained so well, the hand of time, are covered with mementos of its famous hero.

On the further side of this plain, the road, after passing

over a small elevation, reaches the foot of that tremendous mountain, called Mount Altobiscar, which separates France from Spain. The ascent to this is very steep and laborious, and almost impassable for carriages. A ravine descends from this into French Navarre. Our party were leisurely descending into this ravine, hardly anticipating danger, when suddenly our advance guards were stopped by the report of a musket. The alarm was in a moment given, and our arms prepared. On the huge rocks which rose above us a body of men were seen descending, and in a moment they were upon us, preceding their arrival by rolling huge stones down from the mountain, which killed a number of our men.

In a moment we had formed ourselves, as far as the position of the ground would admit, into two squares; and, as they drew near, we discharged our muskets into the midst. Nearly all the foremost fell; but their places were soon supplied by others, who came on with still more force. Their subtle chief was very active in the affray. Fortunately, we had gained a part of the ground where there was a wide shelf, which enabled us to meet the attack more in a body, while the road to it was narrow, and the ground rough. Consequently, they fell fast before our fire. A few minutes only the combat lasted, and yet, on our own side, a hundred men had fallen. Fifty were killed outright; and in several places men and horse had died simultaneously, and so suddenly, that, falling together on their sides, they appeared still alive,—the horse's legs stretched out as in movement, the rider's feet in the stirrups, his bridle in hand, the sword raised to strike, and the expression of the countenance undistorted, but with such a look of resolution and defiance as gave to it a ghastly and supernatural appearance. The loss of the assailants was still greater than ours. Seeing that it would be impossible to attain their object, which was, doubtless, to possess themselves of our baggage, they retired in good order; and, as we considered our charge too valuable to be left in such a spot, we did not attempt to pursue them.

No other incident of interest occurred in our route, and we found ourselves, on the 3rd of June, in safety in Brussels. The next day we reported our arrival to the commanders there; and, on the 5th, our charge was delivered up, and we were inspected, and then ordered to join the garrison which was stationed in Brussels. Here I remained, only performing garrison duty, until that great battle which decided the fate of Europe, and sent the French emperor to his last and lonely home on the barren rock of St. Helena.

CHAPTER 13

Garrisoned in Brussels

These four years thus spent to me were days of quiet, unmarked by aught that would interest my readers; but four years more eventful, more fraught with heavy consequences of good or ill to Europe, have seldom—perhaps never—been numbered in her eventful history. The victorious banners of France were waving on every battle-field on the continent. Wagram and Jena, Austerlitz and Friedland, echoed back the glory of the conqueror's name; and kings and emperors, in whose veins flowed the blood of the Caesars, had esteemed it an honour to claim alliance with the plebeian child of Corsica. But the Russian bear and the English lion had not yet yielded to his claims; and, gathering his vast and victorious armies, he led them to face a sterner enemy and a more subtle foe than they had ever yet contested. Half a million of men, firm and confident in their own resources, had crossed the Niemen under Bonaparte's approving eye.

A few months later, and the remnant of that scattered army, in rags, wan and ghastly, staggered, like a band of spectres, over that same river. No human might had struck them down; but the ice of winter and the deep snows of the north, which the fur-clad Russian glories in, had been the signal of death to the light-hearted child of vine-clad France. He who had left France at the head of such glorious armies had returned to his capital alone with his own brave heart and iron courage, to find there that the arms and gold of the allies had done their work.

From Spain, the French had retreated step by step. Ferdinand, soiled, even in his youth, with flagrant crimes, had returned amid rejoicings and banquets to his capital, to sink still deeper in shame and contempt the Bourbon name, and to reward with dungeons and tears and blood the brave hearts that had struggled so long and nobly for his kingdom. Joseph had fled before him on foot, scarcely escaping with his life from that kingdom, which might, indeed, have taken a glorious place among the nations, had he had the courage or ability to carry out, in the spirit that dictated them, the great and far-seeing plans of his brother.

On every side the nations turned their arms against the falling emperor, until, at length, he who had disposed in his palace of the thrones of Europe had only left one small island, which must have seemed to him but a child's bauble, in view of the past. He *would* not rest here, and the events of the hundred days had roused again the world to arms. The prestige of his name had won back the allegiance of the French, and thousands had, as. in days of yore, collected around his standard.

The battle which should decide the fate of Europe drew on. France stood alone, on the one side, with her veteran troops, and her memories of glorious victories, and, more than all, her emperor; and on the other were the united forces of England and the continent. Napoleon was confident of victory. On the 14th of June, in his own resistless eloquence, he thus addressed his army, the last he was ever destined to command:

"Soldiers, this day is the anniversary of Marengo and Friedland, which twice decided the destiny of Europe. Then, as after the battle of Austerlitz, as after the battle of Wagram, we were too generous. We believed in the oaths and protestations of princes, whom we left on their thrones. Now, however, leagued together, they aim at the independence and the most sacred rights of France. They have committed the most unjust aggressions. Let us, then, march and meet them. Are not we and they still the same men? Soldiers, at Jena, against these same Prussians, now so arrogant, you were one to three; and at Montmirail, one to six. Let those among you who have been captives to the English describe the nature of their prison-ships, and the horrible sufferings they endured. The Saxons, the Belgians, the Hanoverians, the soldiers of the Confederation of the Rhine, lament that they are obliged to use their arms in the cause of princes who are the enemies of justice and the rights of all nations. They know that this coalition is insatiable. After having devoured twelve millions of Poles, twelve millions of Italians, one million of Saxons, and six millions of Belgians, it now wishes to devour the states of the second rank in Germany.

"Madmen! a moment of prosperity has bewildered them! The oppression and humiliation of the French people are beyond their reach; if they enter France, they will find their tomb there! Soldiers, we have forced marches to make, battles to fight, and dangers to encounter; but, if we are firm, victory will be ours. The rights, the honour, the happiness of the country, will be recovered. To every Frenchman who has a heart, the moment is now arrived when he should either conquer or die."

CHAPTER 14

The Waterloo Campaign

The plan which Napoleon had laid down was, by a rapid advance, to force his way between the armies of Wellington and Blucher combined,—to attack one with the mass of his forces, while he detached troops to keep the other in check. Let us now turn our attention to the allies.

They had combined their whole strength at and near Brussels. The army of Blucher, at this time numbered about one hundred thousand men. These occupied Charleroi, Namur, Givet and Liege. The headquarters of the Anglo-Belgian army, under Wellington, were at Brussels. This army numbered seventy-six thousand men; but thirty-five thousand of these, however, were English, the flower of the Peninsular army having been sent to America. The remainder were Hanoverians, Dutch and Belgians. The right of the Prussian army communicated with the left of the English; their commanders having so arranged their troops, that wherever the attack of the French should be made, they might support each other.

They could not doubt that Napoleon's mark was Brussels, but as yet it had been impossible for them to learn by which of the four great routes he intended to force his passage. Several prisoners had been taken, but these either could not or would not communicate the intelligence our commander was so desirous to obtain. On the morning of the

15th, however, the movements of the French unfolded their designs. Their second corps crossed the Sambre, and drove in Zeither's out-posts, who fell back on Fleurus to concentrate with the Prussian corps. They were hastily followed by the French army. The emperor's purpose was then to crush Blucher, before he could concentrate his own forces, much less be assisted by the troops under Wellington.

Immediately Zeither, who had the command at Charleroi, sent out despatches to all the commanders of Blucher's army, summoning them to his aid. Then gallantly marshalling the men who were under his command, they held their ground bravely, though with great loss, until, finding it impossible longer to withstand, they fell back in good order, on a position between Ligny and Armand, where Blucher now awaited Napoleon's attack, at the head of his whole army. Though the emperor's plan of beating the Prussian army in detail had failed, he might still prevent the conjunction of his forces with Wellington's. He continued his march, therefore, on the main road to Brussels from Charleroi. At Frasnes, some Nassau troops had been stationed. These were, however, obliged to retire before the French, who followed them as far as Quatre Bras, or four arms,—a farm, so called because the roads from Charleroi to Brussels, and from Namur to Nivelles, here cross each other. Here the French halted for the night.

Lord Wellington, as I have said, held his headquarters at Brussels. Not a rumour of Napoleon's onward movement had, as yet, reached him. That gay city presented many attractions to our gallant officers, and festivals and parties had followed each other in quick succession. On that very night the Duchess of Richmond gave a splendid ball, and it was as gayly attended by the British officers as if the French had been on the Seine, instead of the Sumbre. Wellington himself was there. Sir Thomas Picton, too, our own brave commander in the Peninsular campaign, who had but that day arrived from England, also met his brother officers in this festal scene.

The festivities were at their height, when an officer in splashed and spattered uniform presented himself at the door, and asking for the duke, communicated to him the startling intelligence. For some moments the iron duke remained in deep reflection, his countenance showing a resolution already taken. Then, in a low and steady voice, he gave a few directions to a staff-officer, and again mingled in the festivities of the hour. But, before the ball was ended, the strains of courtly music were drowned in the louder notes of preparation, The drum had beat to arms, and the bugle summoned the assembly, while the Highland bagpipe added its wild and martial call to the field. All were soon prepared and under arms, and the fifth division filed from the park with the Brunswick corps, and directed their course to the forest of Soignes.

Three o'clock pealed from the steeple-bells. All was now quiet; the brigades, with their artillery and equipage, were gone, the crash of music was heard no longer, the bustle of preparation had ceased, and an ominous and heart-sinking silence succeeded the noise and hurry ever attendant on a departure for the field of battle.

These incidents have been so beautifully described by Byron, that we cannot resist the temptation to quote the passage:

There was a sound of revelry by night,
And Belgium's capital had gathered then,
Her beauty and her chivalry, and bright
The lamps shone o'er fair women and brave men.
A thousand hearts beat happily; and when
Music arose with its voluptuous swell,

Soft eyes looked love to eyes which spake again,
And all went merry as a marriage bell.
But hush! hark! a deep sound strikes like a rising knell.

Did you not hear it? No! 'twas but the wind,
Or the car rattling o'er the stony street;
On with the dance! let joy be unconfined!
No sleep till morn, when youth and pleasure meet,
To chase the glowing hours with flying feet!
But hark! that heavy sound breaks in once more,—
As if the clouds its echo would repeat,—
And nearer, clearer, deadlier than before.
Arm! arm! -it is, it is the cannon's opening roar!

Ah! then, and there was hurrying to and fit,
And gathering tears, and tremblings of distress,
And cheeks all pale, which, but an hour ago,
Blushed at the praise of their own loveliness.
And there were sudden partings, such as press
The life from out young hearts, and choking sighs,
Which ne'er might be repeated;—who could guess
If evermore should meet those mutual eyes,
Since upon night so sweet such awful morn could rise!

By two o'clock the Duke of Wellington had left Brussels, and before light he reached Bry, at which place Blucher was stopping, and there the plan of the day was agreed upon. Napoleon resolved, with his own troops, to attack the Prussian army, because that had concentrated all its strength, while forty-five thousand men, under Ney, were to give battle to the English.

At early dawn, on the 16th, hostilities were renewed. The morning, however, was occupied in slight skirmishes, in which the soldiers in both armies showed their bravery. The main contest between the English and the French commenced about three in the afternoon. The French were drawn up among growing corn, so high as nearly to conceal them from sight. The seventy-ninth and forty-second regiments were thus taken by surprise, and nearly destroyed. Out of eight hundred men, but ninety-six privates and four officers escaped. At night the English general had possession of Quatre Bras. The number of killed and wounded on the side of the allies was five thousand.

Blucher fought as stern a battle, but with less success. He had eighty thousand men, while Napoleon was opposed to him with ninety thousand. The French and Prussians felt for each other a mortal hatred, and little quarter was either asked or given. When the night of the 16th closed around them, thirty-five thousand men were left on the field of battle,—twenty thousand of the Prussians, and fifteen thousand French. Blucher had been forced to retire in the direction of Wavre, and so skilfully were his movements made that it was noon on the 17th before Napoleon discovered his retreat.

As soon as Wellington learned that Blucher had retreated, he gave orders to fall back from Quatre Bras to the field of Waterloo. A heavy rain had fallen all day, and made the roads almost impassable with mud. The English soldiers were wearied with their day's labour, and discouraged by the command to retreat; but their spirits revived when, on reaching their bivouac for the night, they were informed that the battle should be given on the next day.

CHAPTER 15

My Part in the Battle

We found little comfort, however, in our night's position; for, as the darkness closed in, the rain fell in torrents, and was accompanied by heavy thunder.

The soldiers themselves, although no temptation would have been strong enough to have induced them to turn away from the morrow's battle, still could not but feel the solemnity of the hour, thousands of those who had bivouacked with them the preceding night, in health and spirits, were now cold and lifeless on the field of battle. The morrow's action could not be less severe, and in such an hour it was not in human nature to be entirely unmindful of home and friends, whom it was more than probable we should never see again.

For my own part, my thoughts reverted to my dear parents, and I could not but remember that, had I not disregarded their wishes, I should now have been in safety with them. My disobedience appeared to me in a very different light from what it had formerly done; but I resolved to conceal my feelings from every one. I was just endeavouring to compose myself to sleep, when my comrade spoke to me, saying that it was deeply impressed on his mind that he should not survive the morrow; and that he wished to make an arrangement with me, that if he should die and I should survive, I should inform his friends of the circumstances of his death, and that he would do the same for me, in case he should be the survivor. We then exchanged the last letters we had received from home, so that each should have the address of the other's parents. I endeavoured to conceal my own feelings, and cheer his, by reminding him that it was far better to die on the field of glory than from fear; but he turned away from me, and, with a burst of tears, that spoke the deep feelings of his heart, he said, "*My mother.*"

The familiar sound of this precious name, and the sight of his sorrow, completely overcame my attempts at concealment, and we wept together. Perhaps I may as well mention here, that we had not been in the action twenty-five minutes when he was shot down by my side.

After my return to England, I visited his parents, and informed them of the circumstances of his death; and I can assure my readers that it was a painful task. We were not alone in our sad feelings. The fierce contest of the elements, the discomforts of our position, and the deep gloom which covered every object, all served to deepen in every heart those feelings which, I venture to say, even the bravest will experience in the stillness and silence of a night preceding a battle.

With the early dawn of morning all the troops were in motion. Wellington was to commence the action, while Blucher, with all his army, with the exception of a single corps left to contend with Marshal Grouchy, marched to support him.

Our troops were drawn up before the village of Mont St. Jean, about a mile and a half from the small town of Waterloo, on a rising ground, which descended, by a gentle declivity, to a plain a mile in breadth, beyond which rose the opposite heights of La Belle Alliance. The first line was composed of those troops on whose discipline and spirit the duke could most rely. These were the British, three corps of Hanoverians and Belgians, and the men of Brunswick and Nassau. The second line consisted of those whose courage and bravery were more doubtful, and those regiments that had suffered most severely the preceding day. Behind both of these lay the horse. Four roads crossed each other in this position, affording great facilities for the movements of the armies. It included, also, the chateau and houses of Hougomont, and the farm-house and enclosures of La Haye Sainte, which were very strongly occupied, and formed important outworks of defence. The whole front of the British army extended, in all, about a mile.

The army of the French, meanwhile, had been marching all night, and many of them did not reach the heights of La Belle Alliance until late on the morning of the 18th. Napoleon had feared that the English would continue their retreat to Brussels. It was, therefore, with much pleasure that he saw them drawn up on the opposite heights. "At last, then," said he, "at last I have these English in my grasp."

Eighty thousand French soldiers were seen moving, in close massive columns, on the crest of the height, as they took up their several positions for the day. When all was arranged, Bonaparte rode along the lines, reviewing his troops; and when he had finished, and turned to ride away, a loud shout of "*Vive l'Empereur*" rolled after him, which shook the field on which they stood. He then ascended an observatory, a little in the rear, where he could overlook both lines, and from this point directed the battle. It was an eventful hour in the history of this great man; and he felt, as did also his troops, how much depended on the issue of the day. Victory alone would give the courage necessary to send out reinforcements from a country where scarcely any were left but old men and youth. Defeat would be decisive of the emperor's fate. These thoughts nerved the hearts of the French, and they fought with unexampled impetuosity.

About ten o'clock the action was commenced, by an attack upon the gardens and wood of Hougomont. They were particularly anxious to gain this post, as it commanded a large part of the British position. It was furiously and incessantly assailed by the French, and as gallantly defended by the English, under General Byng. The French pushed up to the very walls of the chateau, and thrust their bayonets through the door; but the Coldstream Guards held the courtyard with invincible obstinacy, and the enemy were at length compelled to retire, leaving fourteen hundred men in a little orchard, beside the walls, where it does not seem so many could be laid. Every tree in the wood was pierced with balls, their branches broken and destroyed, and the chateau itself set on fire by the shells.

Travellers inform us that the strokes which proved so fatal to human life have not affected the trees; for, though the holes still remain, their verdure is as beautiful as ever. Beneath those trees, and in the forsaken garden, flowers continue to bloom. The rose-trees and the vines, crushed and torn in the struggle, have flowered in new beauty, and offer a strong contrast to the piles of bones, broken swords, and shattered helmets, that lay scattered among them.

When Napoleon saw that he had failed in taking Hougomont, he strengthened his attack upon the main lines. Most of the British had been drawn up in squares, not quite solid, but several files deep, arid arranged like the squares on a chess-board; so that, if any of the enemy's cavalry should push between the divisions, they could be attacked in the rear, as well as in front. When, therefore, the French artillery opened upon them, and whole ranks were mowed down, the chasms were instantly filled, and not a foot of ground lost. But such was the impetuosity of the French onset, that the light troops, drawn up in front of these squares, were driven in, and the cavalry,' which should have supported them, fled on every side.

The Brunswick infantry now opened their fire upon the French cavalry, with a coolness and intrepidity that made dreadful gaps in their squadrons, and strewed the ground with men and horses that were advancing to the charge. But the courage of the French did not desert them. Their artillery played, at the distance of one hundred and fifty yards, on the British squares, with dreadful execution. Their object was to push back the right wing of the British, and establish themselves on the Nivelles road. But the courage of their opponents rendered these efforts unavailing; and the struggle here at length subsided, to rage with greater fury in other parts of the field.

A strong body of French infantry advanced, without firing a shot, to the position occupied by Sir Thomas Picton and Kempt. They had gained the heights, when Sir Thomas, forming his division into a solid square, advanced to the charge with such effect, that, after firing one volley, the French retreated. That volley, however, proved fatal to our brave commander. A musket ball struck him in the temple, and he expired without a struggle. After his fall, it was ascertained that he had been wounded on the 16th, but had carefully concealed it from every one but his servant. His wound, for want of surgical assistance, had assumed a very serious aspect.

Again the French pressed on, and, attacking the Highland division, drove them back in great disorder. But the brigade of heavy cavalry now came to their assistance, and again the assailants fell back. A column, two thousand strong, bore down upon the 92d regiment, which immediately formed itself into a line, and, charging on the foe, broke their centre. The French were now reinforced by their cavalry, and the British by the brigade of heavy dragoons. A contest then ensued which has hardly a parallel in modern warfare. The determined valour of the British, however, conquered, and the French retired behind their infantry.

It was at this time that Sir William Ponsonby was killed. He led his brigade against the Polish lancers, and took two hundred prisoners; but, riding on in advance of his troops, he entered a newly-ploughed field, when his horse stuck in the mire, and he found it impossible to proceed. At this instant, a body of lancers rode up. Sir William saw that his fate was inevitable. He took out his watch and a picture, and desired some one near to send them to his wife. A moment after, he fell, pierced with seven lance wounds.

At the farm of La Haye Sainte, the French succeeded in cutting off the communication of the German troops stationed there, and put them all to the bayonet. Here they maintained their position, until the final attack in the evening. The combat now raged with unabated fury. Every inch of ground was disputed on both sides, and neither gave way until every means of resistance was exhausted. The field of battle was heaped with the dead; and yet the attack grew more impetuous, and the resistance more obstinate.

The continued reverberations of more than six hundred pieces of artillery, the fire of the light troops, the frequent explosions of caissons blown up by shells, the hissing of balls, the clash of arms, the roar of the charges, and the shouts of the soldiery, produced a commingling of sounds whose effect it would be impossible to describe. Still, the contest raged on. After the advantage gained at La Haye Sainte, Napoleon threw the masses of both infantry and cavalry upon the British centre, which was now exposed. The first battalions gave way under their impetuous attack, and the French cavalry rushed on to carry the guns on the plains. An English ambuscade ran to receive them. The slaughter was horrible. Neither party yielded a step. Three times the French were on the point of forcing their position, and three times they were driven back. They cut to pieces the battalions of the English, who were slow or unskilful in their movements, but could make no impression on the squares. In vain were their repeated attacks. They were repulsed, with the most sanguinary fury.

Napoleon now advanced the whole centre of his infantry, to assist the cavalry. They pressed on with an enthusiasm that overpowered all resistance, and, for the moment, carried all before them. It was at this critical period that our noble commander showed himself worthy of a nation's honour. Everywhere in the thickest of the fight, he was seen cheering by his presence those who were almost ready to fail. He seemed to bear a charmed life. Balls flew thick and fast around him, and his staff-officers fell on every side; yet he moved on unharmed. His unwearied exertions were at length successful in arresting the progress of the French, and in wresting from them the advantages they had gained. Again the attack on the chateau of Hougomont was renewed. The cuirassiers poured the strength of their charge upon the 30th regiment, who received them in a square, and immediately deployed into a line, that the effect of their fire might be more fatal, while the instant re-formation of the square protected them, in a degree, from the next charge of the enemy.

Leaving, at length, the 30th regiment, they rushed on to the 69th, and succeeded in reaching them before their square was formed, which enabled them to commit dreadful slaughter. Before the British cavalry could rush to their relief, only a few brave soldiers remained to effect their escape. Then, retiring to their former position, the fire from three hundred pieces of artillery was poured upon the whole line of the allies. The effect of this fire was very destructive.

One general officer reported to Wellington that his brigade was reduced to one-third of its original numbers, and that a temporary cessation was necessary to the very existence of his troops. "What you propose," was the answer of the duke, "is impossible. You, I, and every Englishman on the field, must die in the spot we now occupy."

"It is enough," replied the general; "I, and every man under my command, are determined to share your fate."

Numerous were the instances on each side, among both officers and men, of self-sacrifice to save their fellow-soldiers. But, notwithstanding the gallant defence of the British, their situation now became critical in the extreme. The first line of their troops had suffered severely, and those brought up to assist them could not always be relied on. One Belgian regiment, which the duke himself was leading to the contest, fled from the first fire, and left the duke to seek for more devoted followers. Another, being ordered to support a charge, was so long in doing it, that the duke sent word to their commander, either to advance immediately, or to draw off his men altogether. He thanked his Grace for the permission, and started for Brussels, alarming the town with a report that the French were at his heels.

The Duke of Wellington felt and expressed the greatest anxiety. He exerted himself to the utmost to cheer his men; but, as he saw how fatal were the French charges, he said to one of the officers near him, "O that night, or Blucher, would come!" Napoleon saw, at last, as he imagined, that the contest was nearly won. Already were couriers sent off to Paris to announce to its anxious multitudes that victory had crowned his efforts. Already had the shouts of "Victory! Victory!" passed from rank to rank among the French, as they saw the lines of the English tremble and fall back. But now a sound was heard which stilled, for a moment, even the fierce tumult of the battle.

It was the voice of the trumpet, announcing the arrival of fresh troops; and the most intense anxiety pervaded every heart, to learn to what army they belonged. Both parties felt that the answer must decide the fate of the day. Marshal Grouchy had been stationed, with thirty thousand men, to control the movements of the Prussian army; and, in case of a severe engagement, he was to advance with his men to assist Napoleon. At daybreak, an aid-de-camp was sent, commanding him to be in readiness at a moment's warning. Soon after, another followed, requesting him to march immediately to the scene of action.

At ten o'clock, he had not moved from his encampment. Still, Napoleon's confidence in him was unshaken. "He has committed a horrible fault," said he; "but he will repair it." Every hour he had expected his arrival; and now, when the first files of the new army emerged from the wood, he felt almost certain that his hopes were realized. But the Prussian standard was unfurled, and the English, with loud cheers and renewed courage, returned to the charge. Even then, Napoleon persisted in believing that the Prussian army was only retreating before the marshal, and that he would soon appear on the field. He was mistaken.

Grouchy, if report may be believed, corrupted by British gold, remained in inglorious safety in his camp. He himself always maintained that he believed the small detachment of the Prussian army which remained near him was the whole of their force; and that, though the very ground under him was shaken by the reverberation of the continued discharges of artillery, he was acting up to his orders in remaining to check the Prussians. Be this as it may, his conduct decided the fate of the day.

The destiny of Europe hung on the feeble intellect of a single man; and his sluggish arm, in its tardy movements, swept crowns and thrones before it, overturned one of the mightiest spirits the world ever nurtured, and set back the day of Europe's final emancipation half a century. In a moment, Napoleon saw that he could not sustain the attack of so many fresh troops, if once allowed to form a junction with the allied forces; and so he determined to stake his fate on one bold cast, and endeavour to pierce the allied centre, with a grand charge of the Old Guard, and thus, throwing himself between the two armies, fight them separately.

For this purpose, the Imperial Guard was called up, which had remained inactive during the whole day, and divided into two immense columns, which were to meet at the British centre. That under Reille no sooner entered the fire than it disappeared like mist. The other was placed under Ney,—the bravest of the brave,—and the order to advance given. Napoleon accompanied them part way down the slope, and, halting for a moment in a hollow, addressed them in his furious, impetuous manner. He told them that the battle rested with them, and he relied on their valour. *'Vive l'Empereur!'* answered him, with a shout that was heard all over the field of battle.

The whole continental struggle exhibited no sublimer spectacle than this last effort of Napoleon to save his sinking empire. Europe had been put upon the plains of Waterloo to be battled for. The greatest military energy and skill the world possessed had been tasked to the utmost during the day. Thrones were tottering on the ensanguined field, and the shadows of fugitive kings flitted through the smoke of battle. Bonaparte's star trembled in the zenith,—now blazing out in its ancient splendour,—now suddenly paling before his anxious eye. At length, when the Prussians appeared on the field, he resolved to stake Europe on one bold throw. He saw his empire rest on a single charge. The intense anxiety with which he watched the advance of that column, and the terrible suspense he suffered when the smoke of battle wrapped it from his sight, and the utter despair of his great heart when the curtain lifted over a fugitive army, and the despairing shriek rung on every side, 'La garde recule,—la garde recule,' make us for a single moment forget all the carnage, in sympathy with his distress.

Nothing could be more imposing than the movement of that grand column to the assault. That guard had never yet recoiled before a human foe, and the allied forces beheld with awe its firm and terrible advance to the final charge. For a moment the batteries stopped playing, and the firing ceased along the British lines, as, without the beating of a drum or the blast of a bugle to cheer their steady courage, they moved in dead silence over the plain. The next moment the artillery opened, and the head of that gallant column seemed to sink into the earth. Rank after rank went down, yet they neither stopped nor faltered. Dissolving squadrons and whole battalions disappearing, one after another, in the destructive fire, affected not their steady courage. The ranks closed up as before, and each treading over his fallen comrade, pressed firmly on. The horse which the gallant Ney rode fell under him; and he had scarcely mounted another, before it also sunk to the earth.

Again and again did that unflinching man feel his steed sink down, until five had been shot under him. Then, with his uniform riddled with bullets, and his face singed and blackened with powder, he marched on foot, with drawn sabre in hand, at the head of his men. In vain did the artillery hurl its storm of fire and lead into that living mass. Up to the very muzzles they pressed, and, driving the artillery-men from their own pieces, pushed on through the English lines. But, at that moment, a file of soldiers, who had lain flat upon the ground behind a low ridge of earth, suddenly arose and poured a volley in their very faces. Another and another followed, till one broad sheet of flame rolled on their bosoms, and in such a fierce and unexpected flow that human courage could not withstand it. They reeled, shook, staggered back, then turned and fled.

Ney was borne back in the refluent tide, and hurried over the field. But for the crowd of fugitives that forced him on, he would have stood alone, and fallen on his footsteps. As it was, disdaining to give way, though the whole army was flying, that noble marshal formed his men into two immense squares, and endeavoured to stem the terrific current; and would have done so, had it not been for the thirty thousand fresh Prussians that pressed upon his exhausted ranks. For a long time, those squares, under the unflinching Ney, stood, and let the artillery plough through them. But the fate of Napoleon was writ, and though Ney doubtless did what no other man in the army could have done, the decree could not be reversed. The star that blazed so brightly over the world went down with honour and in blood, and the ' bravest of the brave' had fought his last battle. It was worthy of his great name; and the charge of the Old Guard at Waterloo, with him at their head, will be pointed to by remotest generations with a shudder.*

* Headley.

195

CHAPTER 16

Wounded

Soon after Sir Robert Picton had received his death wound, while our shattered regiment was charging on the French column, a bullet pierced my left arm, the first wound I ever received in all my engagements,—the mark of which is now plainly visible,—which obliged me to fall back. I bled very freely; and this weakened me so much, that, finding it impossible to continue my retreat over the pile of dead and wounded with which the field was covered, I fell among them.

Here I lay for a few moments, endeavouring to recover my exhausted strength. But here my situation was as dangerous as that of those advancing to the charge. Balls were flying in every direction around me, sometimes striking in the earth, soaked with the recent rains, and throwing it in every direction; but oftener falling on the wounded, who might yet have had a chance for life, and crushing them in a yet more terrible death. Many a poor fellow, who had fallen from wounds, and the weakness induced by exertion, with the loss of blood, was trampled to death by the advancing cavalry.

It was this, combined with an earnest desire to see the progress of the battle, that induced me to endeavour to change my location. I rose, and with great difficulty proceeded but a few steps, when a second ball entered my thigh, which again brought me to the ground. Scarcely had I fallen the second time, when a company of Scotch Greys made a charge upon the French troops, not ten rods from where I lay. I then gave up all hope of ever leaving that battlefield, and expected never to rise again. Already, in imagination, I felt "the iron heel of the horse" trampling out my little remnant of life.

The contest raged fearfully around us. Shots were exchanged thick and fast, and every moment but heightened the horrors of the scene. The blood flowed rapidly from my wounds, and my doom seemed inevitable. An old tattered handkerchief was all that I could procure to stop the rapidly exhausting haemorrhage. With my remaining hand and teeth I succeeded in tearing this into strips, and stuffed it into my wounds with my fingers as best I could. This arrested the crimson tide in some degree. I knew not how severe my wounds might be; but, even if a chance of life remained from them, I knew full well that I was exposed every moment to share the fate of those who lay around me.

Friends and enemies fell on every side, and mingled their groans and blood in one common stream. Our lines were driven back, and our brave men compelled to yield the contest. Rivers of blood were poured out, and regiments of brave men were cut down in rapid succession. Nothing could exceed the bravery of the combatants on both sides. But the French light troops had this advantage of the English,—they could load and fire more rapidly than their enemies.

The duke was compelled to see his plans frustrated, and his lines cut to pieces and driven back by the emperor's troops. Victory seemed already decided against us. Our men were fleeing—the enemy advancing with shouts of victory. The fate of the day seemed settled, and to us soldiers it was so. It was not possible to rally the men to another charge. But, at the moment when all seemed lost, a bugle, with drum and fife, was heard advancing with rapid step. All supposed it to be Grouchy's regiment of fresh troops, ready to follow up the victory, and completely destroy the remnant of the duke's forces.

Consternation now filled every mind, and confusion and disorder reigned. But the Prussian colours were seen hoisted, and it was then announced that Blucher, with thirty thousand men, was at hand. A halt, or rally, and renewed hopes animated every breast. This was the lucky moment, and the fate of the day was at once changed. Report charges Grouchy with being corrupted and bought by English gold, that he sold himself to the allied forces, and thus gave them the victory,—for, had he come at that time, we should have been completely destroyed. Grouchy never entered the fight, or rendered Napoleon any assistance whatever. He was made immensely rich, and spent his life in the English possessions. He has ever been regarded as the man who sold his country and himself to the allies. His life was neither peaceful or happy. He died in 1848.

That Wellington never gained the victory at Waterloo by fair and honourable means, is not and cannot be asserted. But gold accomplished what neither the Iron Duke or his numerous allies could accomplish by military prowess and skill. Napoleon would have gained the victory of Waterloo, had not treachery and bribery done their work. I must own the truth, although it be the lasting disgrace of my nation. I fought hard against Napoleon, and for my king. My hands were both blistered and burned black by holding my gun, which became so hot, the flesh was nearly burnt off the palms of both my hands.

While I lay upon the ground covered with blood, unable to move, some one, more able than the rest, shouted, "The French are retreating. Blucher, with thirty thousand fresh troops has arrived, and is pursuing." This glad sound enabled me to raise my head, and soon, with great joy, I saw that the French were truly falling back, and that our troops were following. Again I felt that I had another chance for life; and this thought gave me strength to reach my knapsack, from which I took a silk handkerchief, and with my teeth and right hand succeeded in tearing it, as I did the one before, and binding up tightly my wounds. This stopped the flow of blood while I remained perfectly still; but the least movement caused it to gush forth afresh.

A little distance from me was a small hill, and under its shelter I should be in comparative safety. O, how I longed to reach it! Again and again I attempted to rise; but every attempt was useless, and I was about resigning myself to my fate, when I observed, only a short distance from me, a woman with a child in her arms.

This woman belonged to the company of camp-followers, who were even now engaged in stripping the dead and wounded, with such eager haste, that they often advanced too near the contending columns, and paid with their lives their thirst for gold. In my travels it has often been my lot to witness the birds of prey hovering over the still living victim, only waiting till its power of resistance is lost, to bury their beaks in the writhing and quivering flesh, to satisfy their thirst for blood. I could think of nothing else, as I saw those wretches, reckless of their own lives, in their anxiety to be first on the ground, and lost to all feelings of humanity for others, stripping from the yet warm dead everything of value upon their persons; not hesitating to punish with death even the least resistance on the part of the wounded, and making sport of their groans and sufferings.

This woman came quite near to me. She stooped to take a gold watch from the pocket of an officer. As she raised herself, a shell struck the child, as it lay sleeping in her arms, and severed its little body completely in two. The shock struck the mother to the ground; but, soon recovering herself, she sat up, gazed a moment upon the disfigured remains of her child, and, apparently unmoved, continued her fiendish work. Thus does war destroy all the finer feelings of the heart, and cherish those passions which quench even the pure flame of a mother's love for her helpless and dependent child. To this woman I appealed for help; and, with her assistance, succeeded in reaching the little hill to which I have alluded, and remained there in safety until the fate of the day was fully decided.

Between eight and nine o'clock that night the last of the French troops had withdrawn from the field, which had been fatal to so many thousands of human beings. The clouds and rain, which had rendered the preceding night so uncomfortable, had disappeared, and the full moon shone in unclouded splendour. The English army, or, at least, that remnant of them left alive, wearied out by the exhausting scenes of the day, had returned to their bivouac of the night preceding, while the Prussians, under Blucher, continued the pursuit of the flying and panic-stricken French.

History informs us that the horrors of that night exceeded even the tremendous scenes of the day. The French were in complete confusion. Carriages and horsemen marched over the fainting and exhausted infantry. The officers tried in vain to rally their men, that they might retreat in order. The first flash of a Prussian gun would scatter them, in the wildest confusion. Thousands fell in the confusion of the retreat, and thousands more were crushed to death, or drowned in crossing the rivers. Napoleon himself but just escaped with his liberty. His carriage was stopped, his postilion and coachman killed, and the door of his coach torn open just in season to witness his escape from the other side.

While Blucher led on the Prussians in this murderous pursuit, the Duke of Wellington again led his army upon the field of battle. The wild tumult and confusion which had pervaded it through the day was now stilled, but the groans of the wounded and the shrieks of the dying were heard on every side. The English re-trod the battle-field, and searched out their wounded comrades, and hastily dressed their wounds. They then constructed litters, and on these carriages were the sick and wounded borne to the hospitals of Brussels and Antwerp.

I have somewhere read a description, written by an eye-witness of the scenes of the night and following day, which I will beg leave of my readers to transcribe here. He says:

The mangled and lifeless bodies were, even then, stripped of every covering—everything of the smallest value was already carried off. The road between Waterloo and Brussels, which passes for nine miles through the forest of Soigny, was choked up with scattered baggage, broken wagons and dead horses. The heavy rains and the great passage upon it rendered it almost impassable, so that it was with extreme difficulty that the carriages containing the wounded could be brought along. The way was lined with unfortunate men, who had crept from the field; and many were unable to go further, and laid down and died. Holes dug by the wayside served as their graves, and the road for weeks afterwards was strewed with the tattered remains of their clothes and accoutrements. In every village and hamlet,—in every part of the country for thirty miles round,—the wounded were found wandering, the Belgian and Dutch stragglers exerting themselves to the utmost to reach their own homes. So great was the number of those needing care, that, notwithstanding the most active exertions, the last were not removed to Brussels until the Thursday following.

The desolation which reigned on the scene of action

cannot be described. The fields of corn were trampled down, and so completely beaten into the mire that they had the appearance of stubble. The ground was completely ploughed up, in many places, with the charge of the cavalry; and the horses' hoofs, deep stamped into the earth, left the traces where many a dreadful struggle had been. The whole field was strewed with the melancholy vestiges of devastation: soldiers' caps, pierced with many a ball,—eagles that had ornamented them,—badges of the legion of honour,—cuirasses' fragments,—broken arms, belts, and scabbards, shreds of tattered cloth, shoes, cartridge-boxes, gloves, Highland bonnets, feathers steeped in mud and gore,—French novels and German testaments,—scattered music belonging to the bands,—packs of cards, and innumerable papers of every description, thrown out of the pockets of the dead, by those who had pillaged them,-—love-letters, and letters from mothers to sons, and from children to parents;—all, all these, and a thousand fold more, that cannot be named, were scattered about in every direction.

The total loss of the allies, during the four days, was sixty-one thousand and five hundred, and of the French forty-one thousand.

For my own part, I was fortunate enough to reach Brussels on the following day; but it was not till the 20th that my wounds could be attended to and dressed. So great was the number requiring surgical attendance, that, although the utmost diligence was used by every surgeon attached to the army, yet many died who might perhaps have been saved, could immediate attention have been given to their wounds.

On this morning, the surgeon came to me, and, having examined my arm, declared that it must be amputated. To this I stoutly refused my consent. He still insisted upon it, saying that it would surely mortify, and cause my death; but I said to him that, if I must die, it should be with my arm attached. My readers may perhaps wonder at my obstinacy; but their astonishment may possibly diminish, when they learn that for *every joint* amputated the operating surgeon obtained an enormous price from the government; and I was confident, in my own mind, that, in my wound, the fee lay at the foundation of his judgment. He persisted, but I was firm; and thus kept my arm, which has since, to my great joy, done me much good service. Others of my comrades in arms were not so fortunate. All day long the business of amputation went on, and at night three carts, laden with legs and arms, were carried away, leaving many hundreds of poor fellows on the invalid list for the remainder of their lives.

CHAPTER 17

A New Life in America

I remained in the hospital at Brussels until September, when orders came that all the invalid soldiers able to be removed should be transported to England. There were four hundred and ninety shipped with myself on board the *Tiger*, and on the 17th day of September we arrived in Chatham. When our ship came into the harbour, we were welcomed with military honours, as soldiers deserving well of their country, and a national salute of sixty-two guns from Fort Pitt heralded our safe arrival in port. I was immediately carried to the hospital, for I was not yet recovered from my wounds, although able to be about part of the time.

Here I remained until the 3rd of December, when I was pronounced cured by the surgeons of the hospital, or so far recovered from my wounds as not to require hospital treatment. My wounds at this time were so nearly healed that I could dress them myself, and I began to feel that I was a man again. I was now ordered to return again to the barracks, and wait until the board should meet to decide upon the disabled soldiers.

I was ordered to Chelsea, into the garrison, under the command of Colonel McCabe, who treated me with great kindness and attention. Here I remained until the 17th of the following May, when orders were received for the invalid soldiers to go before the board for inspection. They did not meet, however, until the 5th day of June, when his Grace the Duke of York, commander-in-chief of the armies of England, convened the board.

Our whole regiment was called, and every man examined; and, reader, how many do you suppose there remained? We were one thousand strong, when we commenced our Peninsular campaign. Only seven men, with our colonel, who had lost one arm, were now alive! Nine hundred and ninety-two had fallen upon the field of mortal strife, and only seven men, beside myself, could be found, in less than one year after the bloody battle of Waterloo! Such, reader, are some of the horrors of war. Nine hundred and ninety-two men, in the prime of life and spirits, out of one thousand, sacrificed to gratify the ambition of kings and nobles!

We passed the board; and what do you think, reader, was the compensation we received for the service we had rendered our country during those years of carnage and blood? One shilling sterling per day! Less than one dollar and fifty cents per week was to be my pay for life, if I remained in Great Britain. Yet even this I was thankful to receive.

I returned, and remained in the garrison at Chelsea, with Colonel McCabe, until March, 1818, when I left to visit Ireland. I was then regularly mustered out of the British army, and returned again to my home, to visit the loved scenes of childhood days, and my ever deaf parents, after an absence of eight years.

For twelve years—that is, until 1830—I remained near my home, when, in consequence of certain things in which I was engaged, I was advised to leave the country with all possible haste. I accordingly petitioned government to commute my pension,—that is, give it up under certain conditions,—and settle in the American provinces. The officers whose duty it was to attend to such business answered that I could receive four years' pay in advance, and two hundred and eighty acres of land in Upper Canada, upon the relinquishment of my pension. These terms were at once accepted by me, and drawing two years' pay in Dublin, I sailed for Quebec. Here I received the remainder of my pay. I immediately proceeded to Montreal, where I took out the deed of my lands, which I now hold. Not feeling perfectly safe in the British provinces, I immediately started for the United States; on entering which, I felt that I was again a free man, and am determined to remain such as long as I live. I came into the immediate vicinity of Worcester, where I have ever since remained; and, by persevering labour, have supported thus far a large family of children. I expect to remain near or in this city, where I shall be happy to see any of my readers, and relate to them any of the incidents of my military life which it was not possible for me to include in the preceding narrative.

In thus closing this brief history of my adventures, I can but look back with regret upon the scenes of strife and bloodshed in which I have been a participator; and if my description of the horrors of these scenes, faint and imperfect though it be, should add but one particle to that broad tide of influence that must be exerted ere the nations of this world shall learn to make war no more, I shall indeed have reason to rejoice, and to pray, with my readers, that that blessed time may soon come, when all this bloody array shall be changed into the peaceful implements of husbandry, and universal love and good-will shall everywhere prevail.

www.ingramcontent.com/pod-product-compliance
Lightning Source LLC
Chambersburg PA
CBHW032057080426
42733CB00006B/316